EXTRAORDINARY Oral Presentations

by Margaret Ryan

Franklin Watts®

A Division of Scholastic Inc.
New York • Toronto • London • Auckland • Sydney
Mexico City • New Delhi • Hong Kong.
• Danbury, Connecticut

EXTRAORDINARY ORAL PRESENTATIONS

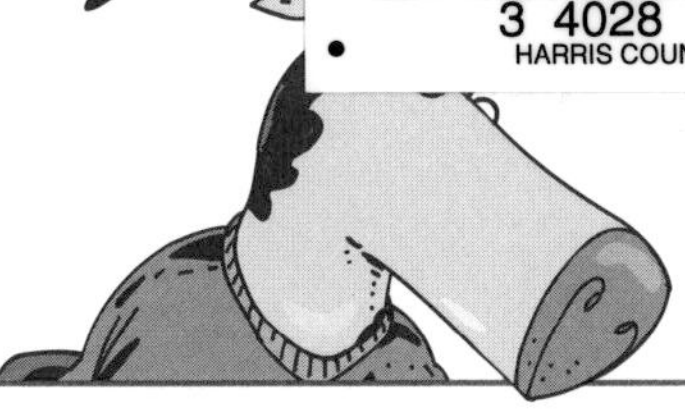

How To Use This Book

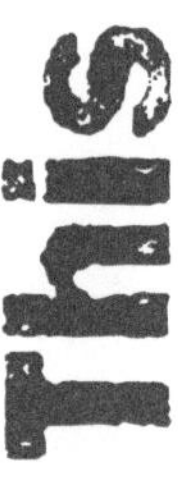

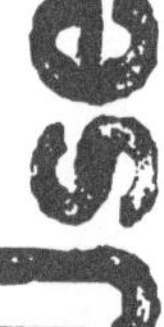

There are lots of extras in this book aimed at helping you create your oral presentation.

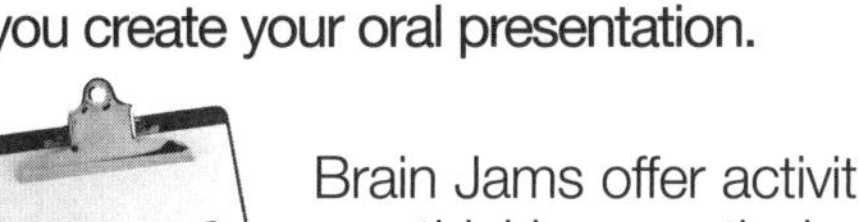

BRAIN JAM

Brain Jams offer activities to get you thinking creatively and give you a chance to hone your skills.

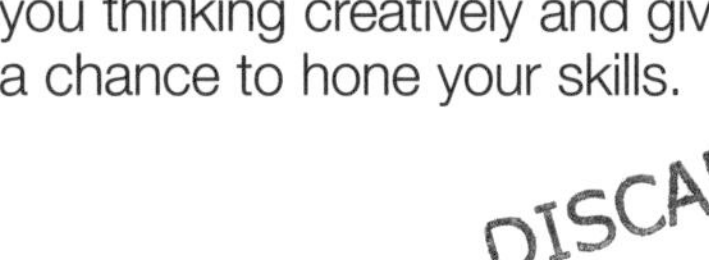

PROJECT JUMP START

Project Jump Starts provide that sometimes necessary extra push to get you going on your own oral presentation.

TIP FILE

Tip Files offer up all sorts of helpful suggestions and hints on getting the project done.

RESOURCES   RESOURCES

One of these icons will lead you to more information.

ORDINARY   EXTRAORDINARY

Throughout the book you will see the ordinary and the extraordinary side by side. With revisions and some thought, these comparisons show you what you can accomplish.

Photographs © 2005: Getty Images: 10 (Evan Agostini), 96 (Hulton Archive); Library of Congress via SODA: 27; Superstock, Inc./National Portrait Gallery: 13.

Cover design: Marie O'Neill
Page design: SimonSays Design!
Cover and interior illustration by Kevin Pope.

Library of Congress Cataloging-in-Publication Data

Ryan, Margaret.
Extraordinary oral presentations / by Margaret Ryan.
p. cm. — (F.W. prep)
Includes bibliographical references and index.
ISBN 0-531-16758-5 (lib. bdg.) 0-531-17577-4 (pbk.)
1. Public speaking. I. Title. II. Series.
PN4129.15.R93 2005
808.5'1—dc22

2005010200

Printed in the United States of America.
1 2 3 4 5 6 7 8 9 10 R 14 13 12 11 10 09 08 07 06 05

HOW-TO MINI-GUIDES

THE BACK MATTER

ASSIGNMENT:

So, you have been assigned to create an oral presentation. No matter the length of your presentation, you will be called upon to use a range of your abilities, such as critical thinking, research, and communication skills.

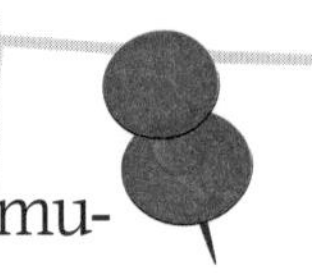

Each state across the country has its own educational plan for you and other students. These plans are called educational standards. From **Oregon** to **New Jersey**, from **North Dakota** to **Florida**, the standards call for students to tackle a variety of oral presentations. In **Pennsylvania**, for instance, eleventh graders are expected to use a variety of sentence structures in their oral presentations. **Nebraska** wants eighth graders to use appropriate gestures, vocabulary, pacing, volume, eye contact, and visual aids in their presentations.

ORAL PRESENTATION

Even if it's not required by your state's standards, learning to give an oral presentation gives you the chance to develop skills that will pay off in your other assignments. Creating EXTRAORDINARY oral presentations includes researching, psyching out your audience, marshalling evidence to make a strong argument, and learning how to hold an audience's attention. You will also develop your artistic skills as you add visuals to your presentation.

So see, you're not alone. As you walk up to begin your presentation, thousands of other students will be doing the same thing. How will you give your project a twist that makes it distinct from all the others? In a word, how do you make it EXTRAORDINARY?

. . . Nebraska is expecting a blizzard of PowerPoint slides . . . To the east, Pennsylvania has been hit by a flood of high-powered creatively structured sentences.

Check Out Your State's Standards!

One way to stay ahead of the game is to take a look at your state's standards for this year and the years ahead. If you're ready to look into your future, try visiting the Developing Educational Standards site at: **http://www.edstandards.org/Standards.html**

On it, you can find links to the educational departments of every state and even focus on language arts in particular.

For more of a national overview of language arts standards, let's take a look at the twelve national educational standards created by the National Council of Teachers of English (NCTE). (For a complete list, visit NCTE's Web site, **http://www.ncte.org.**)

By creating and giving oral presentations, you demonstrate several key skills mentioned in the standards:

- An extraordinary oral presentation indicates that you know how to use spoken and visual language to communicate effectively with a range of audiences and for different purposes.
- An extraordinary oral presentation involves conducting research, posing questions, and probing problems on a topic.
- To create an extraordinary oral presentation you must gather and analyze information from a variety of sources, including technological resources.

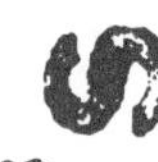

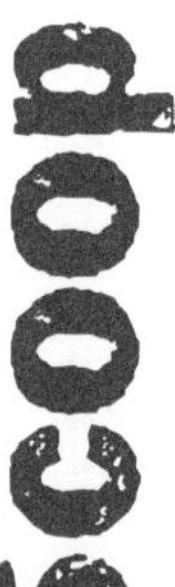

When teachers assign oral presentations, they use a number of factors to determine your grade.

Your speaking ability: Did you speak at an appropriate volume and stress or emphasize words or points? Did you pace your talk appropriately? Did you speak clearly and enunciate your words?

Your physical presence: Did you make eye contact with your audience and use physical gestures during your talk? Are you appropriately dressed and easy to understand?

Your content: Were there enough details, illustrations, and analogies?

Your argument or thesis: Did you develop and support your argument?

Your organization: Did you present information in a logical, interesting sequence the audience could understand?

Your subject knowledge: Did you demonstrate full knowledge of your subject by answering questions with explanations and elaborations?

Your graphics or other visual aids:
Did they enhance and reinforce your presentation?

What's an Oral Presentation Anyway?

A great oral presentation entertains, instructs, informs, amuses, and ideally amazes and impresses. It wins votes, hearts, a good grade, or a contest. Simply put, in an oral presentation, you are presenting information to people by standing before them and speaking. It's not the same as reading a paper aloud; it's more like talking to an audience. And though it's like a speech, it's less formal, shorter, and usually includes some sort of visual tool to help the audience follow along.

For many students (even you, maybe?), the phrase "oral presentation" causes a slight queasy feeling, a wave of dread, or even a surge of panic. This book offers ways to chase away the butterflies and help you give a knockout presentation.

"Surveys show that the number one fear of Americans is public speaking. Death is number two. That means that at a funeral, the average American would rather be in the casket than doing the eulogy." —Jerry Seinfeld (1954–)

Preparation and Practice

Even the most experienced presenters get nervous sometimes. The vice president of a $12 million corporation trembles visibly on his way to the podium each time he has to address a group—about once a week. Famous authors, who have no trouble expressing their opinions on the page, sometimes struggle when it's time to take their ideas to the podium. Anyone who has coached presenters can tell you that there are only two kinds: those who let their fear stop them, and those who take their fear with them and put it to work.

But don't worry. **In at least one way, you're an experienced presentation veteran.** You've seen tons of presentations and speeches before: candidates running for political office asking for votes, the president of the United States speaking on television, your classmates speaking at an assembly. Your school principal probably makes speeches all the time.

What makes the words of one speaker catch your imagination, while those of others put you to sleep? If you're thinking the ability to give a great presentation is simply a gift that some people are born with and that you're doomed to a life of adequate but lifeless presentations, you're wrong.

The making of an extraordinary oral presentation is all about preparation and practice. Great presenters do their homework; they know that practice can lead to an interesting, high-impact presentation. They know the routine, and they follow it.

Here are ten steps for making a great oral presentation.

1. Seek out a great topic or get to know the one assigned to you.
2. Research the facts.
3. Figure out your audience, and work out your angle.
4. Get your facts in order.
5. Make an outline.
6. Write your first draft.
7. Practice your draft.
8. Revise your draft.
9. Finalize your draft.
10. Create supporting visual materials.

As you prepare and give your presentation, you may find some parts of the process easier than others. You might be great at thinking up topics, at researching, or at delivering your talk. Appreciate your strengths and build on them. But don't let the tough stuff throw you. With practice, you can give an extraordinary oral presentation.

"If you have an important point to make, don't try to be subtle or clever. Use a pile driver. Hit the point once. Then come back and hit it again. Then hit it a third time—a tremendous whack."

—Winston Churchill (1874–1965)

So What's an Oral Presentation?

An oral presentation can entertain, instruct, persuade or inform your audience.
An oral presentation . . .

is less formal than a speech and usually includes some sort of visual tool.

takes research, practice, and knowing your audience.

should not be read word for word but spoken from note-cards or outlines.

newspapers

films, music,

azines

commerc

ads and fashi

broadca

chat rooms

overheard convers

HUNT AND GATHER

Finding Your Subject

Finding Your Subject

When teachers hand out oral presentation assignments, they take a variety of approaches, ranging from very restrictive to incredibly flexible. What topic you choose and how you tackle it depends on your assignment. Some teachers pick your topic for you. Some like to give a list of possible topics and let you pick. Still others throw open the doors of the subject vault and tell you to find one on your own.

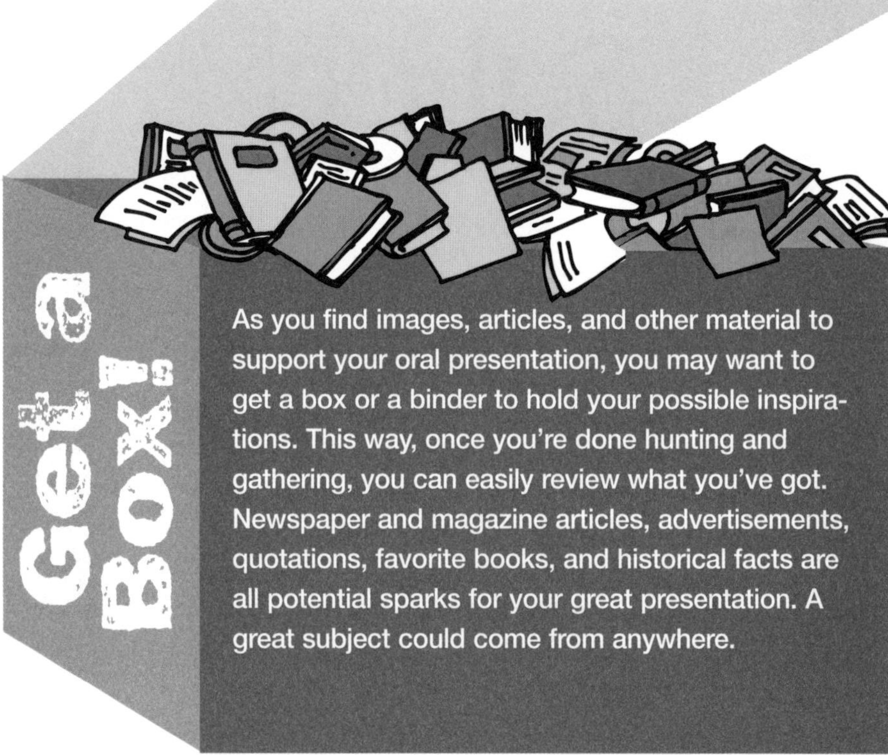

Get a Box!

As you find images, articles, and other material to support your oral presentation, you may want to get a box or a binder to hold your possible inspirations. This way, once you're done hunting and gathering, you can easily review what you've got. Newspaper and magazine articles, advertisements, quotations, favorite books, and historical facts are all potential sparks for your great presentation. A great subject could come from anywhere.

Finding the Wiggle Room in Assigned Topics

Despite your protests, your teacher has decided that you will be the one to speak on the Industrial Revolution. Don't fret yet. Whether it's an assigned topic, such as the Industrial Revolution, or a list of several topics from which you can choose, all assigned topics share a common flaw: They are usually too broad.

Teachers usually assign broad topics on purpose. They want you to have room within the assignment to find an angle that interests you. The most important thing to do with an assigned topic is to narrow it in size. Take a look at the examples below.

Broad Topic	ORDINARY ANGLE	EXTRAORDINARY ANGLE
History of Physics	The Atomic Bomb	Little Boy and Fat Man *or* Hiroshima: What Survivors Say
		Men of the Manhattan Project
		The Enola Gay
	Albert Einstein	It's All Relative
		Einstein in Princeton
My Summer Vacation	The Grand Canyon	Mule Ride to Misery *or* Railroads and the Rim
	A Week at the Beach	Tide Pool with Starfish *or* Mussels and Other Mollusks *or* SPF—What It Means, Why It Matters

As you can see, it's possible to transform a way-too-general topic into something you can cover adequately within your time limit.

When You Choose the Subject

All your teacher did was give you a time limit. Now what? Well, to begin with, talk about something you like. What are your favorite activities, hobbies, movies, books, and sports? Make a list for each of these categories. Pick one item from one of your lists at random, and try it on for size.

Like video games? For history class, you could discuss how games have changed over time, or for your science class, you could look at how the game system works.

Maybe you're interested in animals. For a hot-topic or current-event talk, you could discuss testing pharmaceuticals on animals and why you're for or against it. Have to make a history presentation? How about discussing the evolution of the idea of animal rights? Literature class? Pick a book about animals or veterinarians or a poem about an animal as your topic.

Make lists of things you can't stand. On the other side of the emotional scale, make a list of things you don't like. Whether it's rude people, long lines at the cafeteria, or corporate corruption, write down everything that pops into your head. Don't edit yourself. You'll be doing enough of that later.

Scan the newspaper. Read newspapers, magazines, and online message boards. Look at advertisements, and consider topics such as the latest technology, toys, or trends in fast food. Browse in a bookstore and check out what topics are best sellers in fiction and nonfiction.

What's happening in town? Attend a town meeting or a local organization's event to find out about some of the issues affecting your community. A problem with a railroad bridge might spark a physics presentation, or a debate about traffic signals could lead to a presentation on community laws.

Refine Your Subject, Find a Hook

Every presentation needs a hook to pull in the listener and make it distinct.

If you've narrowed your topic, you're well on your way to finding a core of ideas you can present in a logical manner. For instance, if you're talking about Einstein and you've gotten to "It's All Relative" as your topic, you're going to talk about Einstein's special theory of relativity. But what's your angle? Do you want to view Einstein in the historical perspective and show how he influenced the science that's come after him? Or how Einstein's theory of relativity didn't really have much influence once Niels Bohr and the gang got onto quantum mechanics? Do you want to talk about the "aha!" moment when Einstein realized what he was on to?

Here's a thought: Start with the "aha!" moment. It's an emotion-grabber. Or begin with Einstein alone in his second-floor study in Princeton, trying to work out his grand theory of everything and failing (another emotion-grabber). Then look back on his amazing work on relativity. Oh, and be sure you define relativity for the layperson in a couple of sentences.

What's Your Main Point: That Is, Your Thesis?

Well, it's either one of two points of view:

A. Einstein's theory of relativity influenced all the physics work that has followed.

B. Einstein's theory of relativity, while a stunning piece of scientific thought, became somewhat irrelevant with the development of quantum mechanics.

Pick either one as your thesis statement, and you'll know which opening to choose. If you're choosing A, start with the "Aha!" moment. If you're choosing B, begin with the scenario in Princeton. One speaks of triumph, the other of frustration. You've found a hook for your talk. And opening with drama, tragedy, and color should keep your audience interested long enough for them to learn a little something.

Using Your Personal Experiences As a Subject

For personal experiences, you want your thesis to convey what you learned from your experience or any new insights you gained. Let's say you've decided to talk about that summer vacation. "We went to the Grand Canyon and it was a big hole in the ground" could easily become "Mule ride to misery—here is my dim view of that daylong journey to the bottom." What lessons did you learn as you rode that mule? What insights did you gain into your family members, geology, the soul of a mule, or yourself?

Take the Thesis Less Traveled

You've been assigned to do an oral presentation on the poet Sylvia Plath for English class and read that she committed suicide at the age of thirty. What influence did her tragic death have on the success of her poetry? Is her work that good, or is it the dramatic ending of her life that still sparks people's interest in it? Whatever you decide, you can use that as your hook: "Plath's work is still read only because of the romantic notion that poets must be insane." Or "Plath's work is better than the hype. Forget the bio—read the book."

Looking at the personal life and experiences of a subject is a great way to find a fresh approach. For a history assignment, you might have to do a presentation on Abraham Lincoln's Gettysburg Address. Nearly everyone knows how it begins: "*Four score and seven years ago . . .* " But how many people know that Lincoln's audience thought the speech was a flop? You might want to look at how his life or personality influenced the type of speaker he was. A new angle is not hard to find as long as you keep your eyes open for unusual information.

The important thing in creating your thesis is taking a stand. Give your topic a personal slant—an angle that appeals to you—but make sure it's something you can argue. Don't make it something everyone agrees on, like "the sky is blue" or "school stinks." You'll have a hard time with those types of topics. If your thesis is a little controversial, that's okay. In fact, it's terrific. That way, you can be sure you'll keep your audience awake.

Theses: From Ordinary to Extraordinary

A strong thesis has a distinctive point of view. It also provides some insight or reasoning for the position.

ORDINARY	EXTRAORDINARY
The death penalty is cruel and unusual punishment.	With DNA evidence calling many guilty verdicts into question, the death penalty may be against the Constitution.
Land pollution is destroying the planet Earth.	Caused by more than just trash on the ground, land pollution is wrecking Earth's soil.

Your next step is to gather information to support your thesis. Keep an open mind while you research; you may discover facts that will cause you to rethink your position.

BRAIN JAM:

Create a Brainstorm!

Draw it out. Try writing the potential subject on paper. Now circle it and write things you associate with it nearby, and circle them as well. Draw lines connecting them to the original subject. Write words and phrases related to these new ideas, branching out as you go. Work until you fill the page. The more ideas you get on paper, the better the odds you'll hit the topic jackpot.

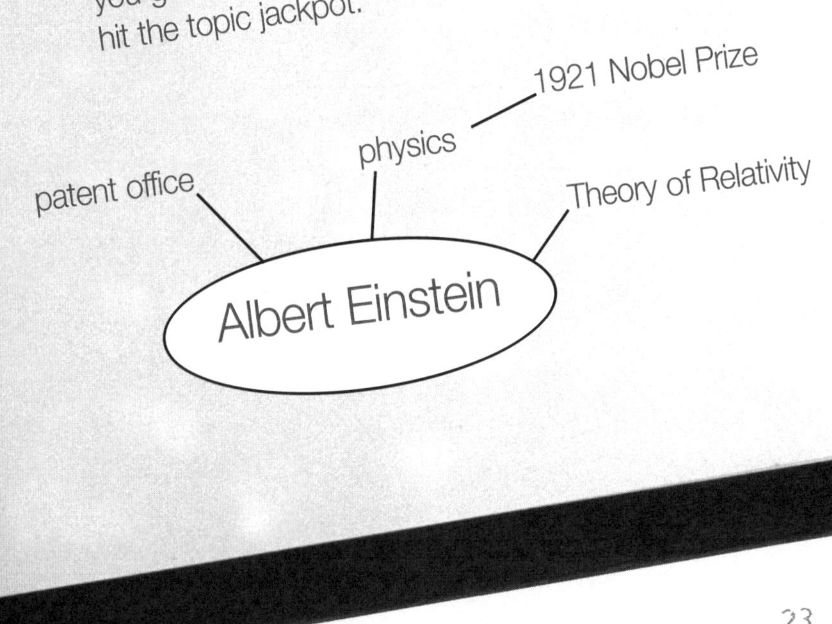

Anecdotes and Books

THE VISION

Support Your View with Research

Support Your View with Research

Presentations aren't just about what you think; they're about what you can prove. Support your statements with facts, anecdotes, and examples if you want to be persuasive and interesting. Here are some ideas on how to find the facts, quotations, anecdotes, and humor that will bring your presentation to life.

Where to Find Information

Begin your treasure hunt at home. Gather books and magazines you can use in a single place at home. Don't forget about pictures, diaries, and family histories; these can be fabulous materials too.

Turn on a computer. You can use a search engine like **Google** to help find information about your topic. If you're doing a presentation on the West Nile Virus, you'll want to check out the information available on the Centers for Disease Control and Prevention's site (**http://www.cdc.gov**). If you've picked Edgar Allan Poe, try the Web site for the Edgar Allan Poe Museum in Richmond, Virginia (**http://www.poemuseum.org**). For English class presentations, you might want to visit **http://www.bartleby.com**, which offers access to the full text of a number of famous works.

Tap your local resource. Anyone can go to a library and check out what's on the shelves, but how many people ask their librarian or media specialist for help? Discuss your topic with a librarian. Librarians are trained to know how to find information and will most likely be glad to help you explore books, magazines, academic journals, microfilm, video collections, and more. He or she may help you make some interesting discoveries about your subject.

Check your library's online resources. Many libraries offer access to magazines, journals, and databases online. Some let you read articles, or even whole books, right at the computer. Others tell you where to find articles and books about your subject.

Access online databases. These are filled with articles and encyclopedia entries. For example, the **Academic Search Premier** database provides full text for 3,288 scholarly publications covering academic areas of study, including social sciences, humanities, education, computer sciences, engineering, language and linguistics, arts and literature, medical sciences, and ethnic studies. **Encyclopedia Americana** is available in an online version, which has an added news database.

"Get the facts first, and then you can distort them as much as you please."
—Mark Twain (1835–1910)

When to Trust a Web Site

Not everything you read on the Internet is true. Both amateurs and experts in their fields, for example, can create official-looking Web sites. It's better to double-check your facts than discover you've made a blunder in the middle of your presentation.

What does the Web address end with? Is it .gov, .edu, .org, .biz, .net, or .com?

- In general, Web sites ending in **.edu** are educational institutions and are often the most reliable.
- Web sites ending in **.gov** are associated with the government and can be sources of statistics and other government data. But be aware that the "government" is made up of people who have prejudices, too.
- Sites ending in **.org** tend to be nonprofit organizations, which might be more trustworthy than for-profit sites with things to sell. However, they may be skewed to advance their specific causes.
- Web sites ending with **.biz** or **.com** are usually selling something, so their facts may be altered to encourage you to buy something.

No matter what site you use, proceed with care. Many reporters use at least three sources to confirm a piece of information. You want to make sure your facts are facts, not someone else's fiction.

Finding Quotations

Along with all of the fabulous facts, you may want to find quotations to use in your presentation. **Quotations make great openings, closings, and transitions.** That's why good presenters use them so often. Consider how you might use the following quotes in a presentation.

"If you make every game a life and death proposition, you're going to have problems. For one thing, you'll be dead a lot."

—Dean Smith, basketball coach

"Sour, sweet, bitter, pungent—all must be tasted."

—Chinese proverb

"You do not lead by hitting people over the head—that's assault, not leadership."

—Dwight D. Eisenhower,
U.S. president, 1953–1961

Imagine opening with one of these catchy quotations. A powerful quotation can add punch to any presentation. So, where do you find them?

Bartlett's Familiar Quotations is still the standard source. It's available at bookstores and libraries in updated editions and online through **http://www.bartleby.com.**

You can also try doing an Internet search on "quotations about _____." You'll be led to a variety of sites. Poke around and see what you discover.

When you're looking for quotations, give yourself time. It's important to read around and find one that works exactly. You can always begin with ***Bartlett's Familiar Quotations***, but the quotations in it are long and sometimes obscure.

Here are some other good places to find quotations on the Internet:

- **The Quotes and Sayings database** links to other quotation sites on the Internet and lets you search quickly through a number of resources. **http://www.quotesandsayings.com**

- **Creative Quotations:** search fifty thousand quotations (and biographical information) for more than three thousand famous people. This is a great research tool for students, teachers, and quotation lovers. **http://creativequotations.com**

- **The Quotations Page** is the one of the oldest quotation sites on the Internet, and still one of the best. **http://www.quotationspage.com**

Anecdotes

Anecdotes—very short stories—can add energy to your remarks. They can be humorous, emotional, or serious. Look for anecdotes that make a point quickly and that fit in with the rest of your presentation. You want the anecdote to support your point, not serve as a diversion from it.

When you're looking for an anecdote, start by deciding what purpose you want it to serve. The best anecdotes are based on personal experience, but don't let that limit you. There are many sources of anecdotes, including an almost endless variety of Internet sites.

BARTLETT'S BOOK OF ANECDOTES

by Andrés Bernard and Clifton Fadiman is a great reference. You can also look for a book of anecdotes directly related to your subject. There are collections of anecdotes about almost everything—New York City, Judy Garland, artists, architecture—the list goes on and on.

Humor

Humorous quotations and jokes are a great way to lighten up your presentation. But it's sometimes hard to find a good joke when you need one, especially one that you can tell in front of your teacher. But there are plenty of sources of humor you can use for inspiration.

Watching television can give you some ideas. Late-night comics usually begin their shows with a monologue. If you can catch one or two, you'll get a sense of how to make jokes about current events. There are also numerous publications and Web sites that specialize in humor. ***The Onion,*** which does an excellent job of creating funny fake news articles, is available free in many towns and online.

Books

Encyclopedias, dictionaries, and other reference books are great for finding brief overviews of a subject or for looking up the meaning of specific terms. ***The New Princeton Encyclopedia of Poetry and Poetics*** will help you define pastoral poetry, for example, while the ***Columbia Encyclopedia*** will give you a brief article on the life and times of the poet John Milton. Use sources like these to get an overview or to help define terms.

In general, look for books with recent publication dates—say, within the last three to five years. For current events, even this may be outdated. But if you're working on a history presentation on the French and Indian War, you might be able to find a memoir written by someone who witnessed it. A direct quotation describing one of the battles could go a long way toward helping your presentation.

The Power of Primary Sources

A primary source is the thing itself—the book written by its author, an eyewitness account of a battle, a document such as the **Declaration of Independence**, or an autobiography. It's direct information, unlike a secondary source.

A secondary source is a comment on the thing itself—a work of literary criticism, a historian's account of a battle pieced together from several eyewitness accounts, a discussion of the **Declaration of Independence**, or a biography. Many teachers require you to use primary sources in your reports, essays, and other research projects because they are so important.

Extraordinary Sources

We've covered most of the typical research resources, but here are four you may not have tried yet:

Audio and Video Sources

Remember, CDs, DVDs, and videotapes are research material, too. Just because you don't read them doesn't mean you can't use them. Check libraries, video rental stores, and online stores, such as **amazon.com** or even **netflix.com,** to see what material is available on your subject. Also check on the Web sites of some television channels with an educational focus, such as the **History Channel, National Geographic,** or **Discovery,** for suitable programs.

Personal Research

For a science project, you might propose a hypothesis and test it, keeping notes on your experiments and findings. This would become the heart of your presentation. For a history project, you might interview eyewitnesses or locate and study original documents, and then present your findings.

Interviews

You can base an entire talk on interviews. Let's say your topic is human rights abuses in China. Do you know anyone from China? No? Well, do you know anyone who knows anyone from China? Is there a local cultural organization you can contact? Once you start asking around, you'll be surprised by who turns up.

Once you've found a willing interviewee, it's time to do a little legwork. To get a great interview, do your homework on the topic, and know this person's relationship to it. Was this person jailed for his political beliefs? Knowing something about your subject shows him or her respect.

Keep in mind that an interview is a conversation with a purpose. It's important to have at least five questions ready to begin your interview. Ask open-ended questions, not, "Do you believe you were treated unfairly?" Rather, ask "How do you feel your human rights were violated?" Don't be afraid to deviate from your script. Ask follow-up questions, even if they were not on your list.

Polls

You can create your own data by taking a poll. Let's say you're researching a proposed plan to do random drug testing of students in your school. Create a short questionnaire and ask as many students as possible what they think of the idea. Do they approve or disapprove, and why?

Be sure you let your audience know how many people you interviewed, who they were, and what percentage thought one way or the other. For example: *"Seventy-five percent of the students I spoke with—a total of four hundred juniors and seniors—said they would vigorously support random drug testing in our high school. Why? Well, the reason most often cited was . . . "*

Taking Notes, Revisited

Having all of the greatest information in the world won't help you if you don't have a way to organize it and find it later when you need it. The reason note cards (also called index cards) are still around and haven't gone the way of the typewriter is because they are extremely useful. When taking notes:

- ✓ Use one card for each idea, fact, or quotation.
- ✓ Choose a size that's small enough to carry around and handle easily, but big enough to write on. A 4-inch by 6-inch or 5-inch by 8-inch card should work well.
- ✓ Write notes on one side of the card only. This will save you time when you are looking for a fact—it won't be on the back of any card.
- ✓ Write down the source of the information, which is bibliographical material, in case you need to credit the source or find it again.

Sample Note Cards

Here are some sample note cards you might prepare for a presentation on how governments are trying to limit teenage drinking.

To crack down on teenage drinking, the Russian parliament passed a law banning drinking in stadiums, streets, parks, and other public places except restaurants. Beer ads are also banned from airing on TV before 10 P.M., and they carry mandated health warnings.

BusinessWeek, 11/15/2004,
"No Beer for You, Boychik" by Jason Bush

A study by the Center on Alcohol Marketing and Youth [researching popular magazines] . . . found that underage youths saw more alcohol advertising than did adults in 2002, and teen girls were far more likely to be exposed to advertising than teen boys.

"The new face of underage drinking: teenage girls" by Armstrong, Elizabeth; McCarroll, Christina.
Christian Science Monitor, 7/8/2004, Vol. 96, Issue 156

In states with tougher and more restrictive licensing laws, young drivers had lower rates of heavy drinking and driving, according to a study by the Substance Abuse and Mental Health Services Administration.

USA Today Magazine, Nov 2004, vol. 133,
Issue 2714, p. 8

So what makes for extraordinary notes? Well, knowing when to copy down word for word and when to paraphrase is a good place to start. Summarizing concepts or definitions in your own words will help you get more comfortable with your subject. Anything specific like a fact or a quotation should be written down as it is written. You'll also want to keep a running list of all of the sources you used, which is called a bibliography; you may be asked to hand it in.

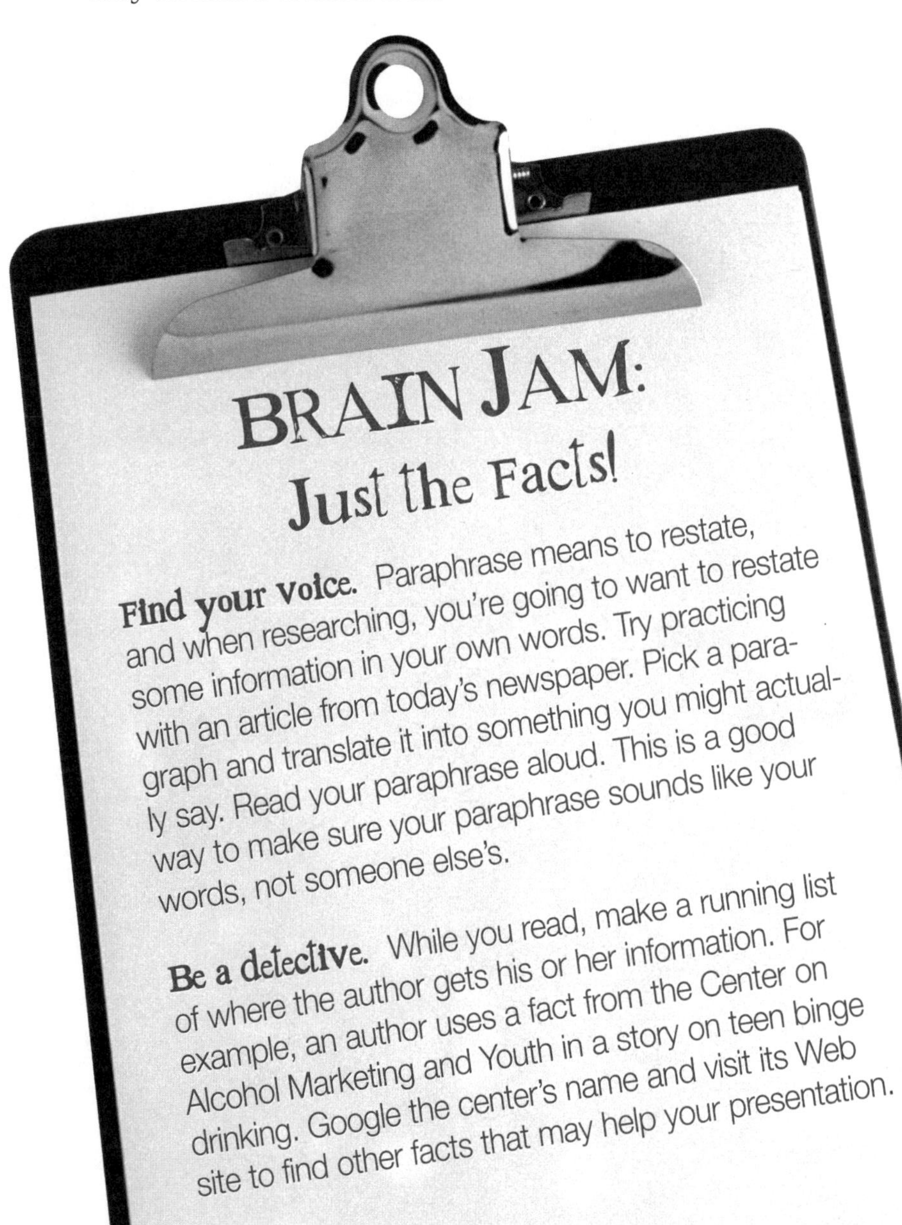

review your

Consider your

Pick a

create a draft

CREATIVE CONSTRUCTION

Assemble Your First Draft

Assemble Your First Draft

You've got a topic and an angle, and you have done a lot of research. But have you thought about your audience? Believe it or not, that's the most important factor in creating an oral presentation that sings. So take some time to think about who you are talking to.

- **Is it a large group or a small one?** Small groups are more intimate and make it easier for people in the audience to ask questions.
- **What does the audience already know about your topic?** Do you need to establish that Einstein was a physicist, or can you get right into the intricacies of relativity?
- **What issues and concerns, if any, will the audience have about your topic?** Can you address these?
- **What technical terms, or jargon, will be unfamiliar to the audience?** Do you have to explain that GUI stands for "graphical user interface," or will your audience already know?
- **When will you be speaking?** Where will you be in the program? First and last speakers are always the most memorable.
- **Is it a captive audience?** That is, do they have to attend? If so, you may find them blasé and bored. Make sure what you say is really interesting.

Be Ready for Challenges

Once you've thought about your audience—how familiar they are with your topic or how well you expect them to understand what you're talking about—list three major challenges to their understanding of the ideas you'll present. For instance, if you are talking to the third grade about Einstein, a challenge might be, "They've never heard of Einstein." If you're talking to parents about the right of athletes to use steroids, a challenge might be, "They're opposed to any and all illegal drug use."

What three challenges can you anticipate? What strategies can you come up with to help you overcome these challenges? If, for example, your audience will be unfamiliar with the terms used to discuss your subject, you can define them briefly at the beginning of your presentation.

TIP FILE

WIIFM is an acronym that stands for "what's in it for me?" That's what everyone in your audience will be asking. What can I get out of this? Give them something—even if it's only hints on how to give an awesome presentation.

Begin Building Your Presentation

It's time to start constructing your presentation. Every presentation has a simple structure, made of three parts just like a sandwich:

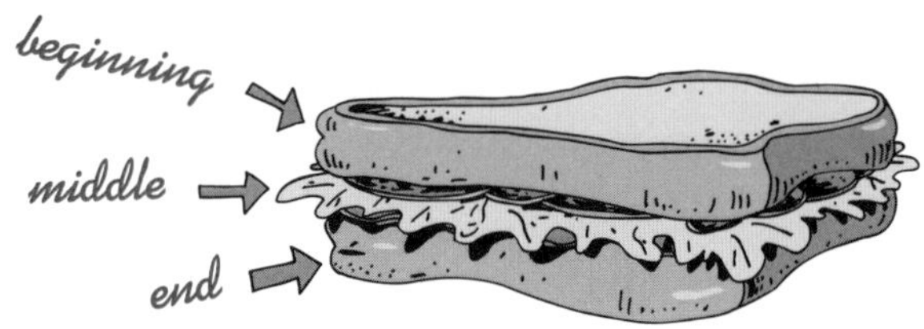

- The beginning introduces the topic.
- The middle talks about the topic.
- The end summarizes the topic.

Or, as the well-worn saying goes,
"Tell them what you're going to tell them.
Tell them. Then tell them what you told them."

Writing a Great Opening

Writing a great opening can be one of the hardest parts of getting your presentation in shape. So write a rough one now and plan on revising it later. When you're ready to create your opening, think about its purpose.

The opening of an oral presentation has to:

- get the attention of the audience.
- establish your credibility.
- arouse curiosity.
- inform by presenting the thesis statement.
- help you begin with confidence and enthusiasm.

Mastering the Middle: Informative or Persuasive Presentations

Deciding how your information should be structured can be a challenge. There are two basic types of oral presentations: **informative presentations** and **persuasive presentations.** Take a look at these and see which one works for you.

Informative Presentations

Speeches designed to inform come in many flavors. You might be explaining concepts, laying out principles, telling about rules and procedures, or explaining processes.

On the other hand, you might be describing an object—a chambered nautilus shell or the skull of a beaver in science class, for example. You could be telling about a person—George Washington Carver or a character in a book. You might be telling about a place—your vacation in Yosemite—or telling about events and historical developments—the growth of the Internet or the invention of the telephone.

Note to Self:
Create oral presentation to inform using cause and effect, chronology, geographic order, or other organizing structure

Time allotted: 15 minutes

Here are some ways to organize a presentation designed to inform:

Cause and Effect

What events led up to the current situation? If you're talking about the development of alternative sources of energy, you could tell your audience about the Arab oil embargo of the 1970s, which led to a shortage of oil and higher fuel prices. You could talk about how the war in Iraq and aggressive oil trading are fueling higher prices today, and why the situation calls for incentives to develop solar, wind, and water power.

Chronology

Are you tracing the history of an idea or the development of an attitude or situation? Use chronology—the order in which the events took place in time. Talks about the designated hitter, the development of robotics, or the growth cycle of a redwood tree would all benefit from the use of chronological ordering. It's easy to do. After all, in history, A.D. 1067 always comes after 1066. And most people know that trees start as seeds, and that the Great Depression came before World War II, and that postwar prosperity led to the Baby Boom.

Geographic Order

Talking about the breakup of the Soviet Union or your family's trip across the country? Geographic order can help. Begin in the north and work your way south or start in the east and work your way west, or vice versa. Make sure you announce your plan: "Let me begin with the northern region, and then work my way south."

Quantitative Order

If you are discussing the ten biggest diamond deposits on Earth, **you can start with the largest and work toward the smallest, or vice versa.** In general, it's best to work your way up, so you end with the most impressive. Start at the top, and your audience knows there's no place to go but down. Start small, and excitement can build as you talk.

Persuasive Presentations

A presentation to persuade involves laying out a convincing argument backed up with evidence to lead your audience to a specific conclusion.

If the point of your presentation is to persuade, then consider the following:

Criteria/Satisfaction

Begin by setting up the criteria for making a certain decision—that is, based on what information would a reasonable person make this choice? Let's say you're arguing in favor of a candidate for school office. You might start by outlining the traits of the ideal candidate. Then tell your classmates why Emma Baker fits the description. You can use this form to persuade an audience why a certain person, object, philosophy, or event is the one to choose.

Urge to Action

In some ways, **a persuasive presentation can be seen as a type of sales pitch.** You want to convince your audience to do something. Below is a proven method used by sales professionals for getting people to act.

- First, get your audience's attention with a stunning opening.
- Next, show them that there is a need that affects them. Outline a problem that needs fixing. Tell them about a situation that needs to change. Use both emotion and logic to establish the need.
- Once you've established the need, satisfy it. Present a solution to the problem. Then show your plan, your candidate, your product, and why it will work. Use logic to establish this point.
- Next, help the audience visualize how much better things will be if they do what you're asking.
- Ask for action. Be specific. Buy our product. Vote for Joan. Stop teen drinking now. Call your congressperson.
- Once you've asked for the action, stop talking. If you go on longer, you'll only weaken your pitch.

Problem/Solution

Another way to organize the persuasive talk is to **lay out the problem in some detail, then propose your solution.** When giving solutions, try to anticipate objections. Imagine someone in the audience saying that your idea won't work, for a certain reason, and work your rebuttal to that point into your presentation.

Refute an Idea

How would you convince an audience that an idea they hold dear is really quite wrong?

- **State the point and tell why it's important.** Explain how you will refute the point.
- **Point out any fallacies in the reasoning** that supports the idea you are against. Present evidence that contradicts the idea.
- **Show how the opposition's evidence is false.** To close, show how you have discredited the position of the opposition.

The End: Tell Them What You Told Them

This is the time to wrap it all up for your audience. First, you want to quickly summarize what you covered in your talk. Take your original thesis and modify it based on the evidence you've just been presenting.

As for your absolutely last words, you'll want them to be memorable. That's why many presentations close with:

an anecdote.

a powerful fact.

a positive statement about the future.

a quotation.

Don't worry if you can't think of a killer closing yet. You'll be able to work on it more as you put together your outline and refine your draft.

Jump-Start Your Outline

Look at your notecards. Now that you have a general organizational approach in mind, take another look at your note cards. Read through them slowly. Does anything seem like opening material to you? Does anything seem like it might make a good closing? Put those cards aside. This is just a rough sort. We'll refine the choices later.

Summarize them. Now go through your remaining cards, and on a fresh card write a sentence that summarizes each. For example, you might summarize the cards from page 36 this way:

To crack down on teenage drinking, the Russian parliament passed a law banning drinking in stadiums, streets, parks, and other public places except restaurants. Beer ads are also banned from airing on TV before 10 P.M., and they carry mandated health warnings.

BusinessWeek, 11/15/2004,
"No Beer for You, Boychik" by Jason Bush

Summary:

In Russia, laws are being passed to limit teen drinking.

A study by the Center on Alcohol Marketing and Youth [researching popular magazines] . . . found that underage youths saw more alcohol advertising than did adults in 2002, and teen girls were far more likely to be exposed to advertising than teen boys.

"The new face of underage drinking: teenage girls" by Armstrong, Elizabeth; McCarroll, Christina.
Christian Science Monitor, 7/8/2004, Vol. 96, Issue 156

Summary:

Teenagers see more magazine ads for alcohol than adults do.

In states with tougher and more restrictive licensing laws, young drivers had lower rates of heavy drinking and driving, according to a study by the Substance Abuse and Mental Health Services Administration.

USA Today Magazine, Nov 2004, vol. 133, Issue 2714, p. 8

Summary:

Fewer young people drink and drive in states with tougher licensing laws.

Read your new cards. Once you've got these new cards together, put aside the old deck. Now read your new cards, and order and reorder them until a story starts to emerge.

Write or type out your main points. This process takes time and thought. It's like putting together the pieces of a jigsaw puzzle until the picture starts to emerge. It sometimes takes a while for this picture to become clear, but be patient. This is the heart of the creation process. Alternatively, you can try using the outlining feature on a program such as PowerPoint to help you get your ideas in order.

Once you've got the order worked out, this is the beginning of your outline. Write or type out the main points, filling in details from the original note cards to prove each point:

SAMPLE SUMMARY

MAIN POINTS

Teens are encouraged to drink by the media.

- No liquor ads on TV
- But teens see more ads in magazines than adults do—fact
- Movies also glorify drinking—example

Countries around the world are passing laws to try to limit teen drinking.

- Laws in Russia, France, the United States

These laws seem to be working.

- Statistics on the effect of tougher state licensing laws

As Easy As 1, 2, 3

Creating an outline can basically be broken down into three steps:

1 Go through your note cards and create generalized statements from each fact. That is, broaden out from a particular fact to a general idea or concept.

2 Arrange your concepts in a logical manner, following the organizational pattern you chose.

3 Go back and support each assertion with evidence gathered in your research.

Now all you need is an opening and a closing. For your rough draft, don't worry too much about getting these elements perfect. You'll be able to test and refine them as you practice.

Smooth Transitions

In your draft, you mapped out the middle, or bulk, of your presentation. But even if you have all your thoughts in order, remember that **your audience will need to be led gracefully from one point to the next.**

In a written report, readers can see and record your transitions on the page. In an oral presentation, listeners will need to be reminded from time to time of where you are in the presentation, what you've said already, and what you'll say next.

Think of transitions as signposts and bridges. They tell your audience where you are and lead them ahead to the next topic. Good transitions, like good openings, are often added after the first draft of your outline or script exists. As you read through your notes, mark places where you need to add a transitional word, phrase, or idea.

A Sample Outline to Get You Going

Let's walk through this blueprint for an informative speech outline.

INFORMATIVE SPEECH

SAMPLE OUTLINE

I. Thesis Statement

Write your statement here.

II. Introduction

A. **Start with an attention-grabber:** Will you begin with a quotation, anecdote, joke, fact, or other opener?

B. **Motivate the audience:** Let your audience know why the topic matters. Why should they pay attention to you? *(Teen drinking and driving is a serious issue that affects every one of us.)*

C. **Establish credibility:** Why are you speaking on this topic? If you have special experience or knowledge, tell the audience here.

D. **Preview main points:** Write out your thesis statement so that you preview each of your main points. *(Today, I'm going to talk about how governments are trying to prevent teen drinking and driving by passing laws, and how those laws are working.)*

Transition: Write out your transition. How will you leave the introduction and begin the body? (Review the transition strategies listed on page 63.)

SAMPLE OUTLINE

CONTINUED

III. Body

Point one. Write a phrase to indicate the first point you'll discuss. List your support material as subpoints. Provide the name of the source from which the support material came. Put quotation marks around direct quotes and list the name of the book or magazine where you found the data. (*BusinessWeek*, Nov 15, 2004.)

Transition: Write out your transition. Indicate with a transition that you are discussing the next main point.

Point two. Your next main point.

Transition: Write out your transition. Indicate with a transition that you are discussing the next main point.

Point three. Your next main point.

Transition: Write out your last transition. Indicate with a transition that you are beginning the conclusion of your speech.

IV. Conclusion

A. Review. Tell the audience what you told them. Provide them with a brief explanation of what you said.

B. Summarize shortly. End with a strong closing. Finish a story, end with another fact, or close with a quotation.

Why Practice Yo

Test out your pre

Revisit and revis

mprove your deliv

et comfortable with

watch your bod

THINK OUT OF THE BOX

Practice Your Way to a Final Draft

Practice Your Way to a Final Draft

One of the most crucial steps in creating an extraordinary oral presentation is practicing. Read your presentation out loud at least three times. Read slowly, and speak clearly. Most people speak much faster than most audiences can handle, so slow down.

Note where your voice should be louder or softer and where it makes sense to slow down, speed up, or repeat a point.

Look for places to add visual or even audio supporting materials. Visuals can help you get your point across and are often expected to be part of a presentation.

Try a Test Run

After you've gone through your presentation a few times on your own, it's time to gather friends or relatives to be your audience.

As you begin, speak slowly and clearly, with expression. No reading! Work from note cards, memorize your presentation, or use visual aids to help you remember your main points.

Along with managing your voice:

- **Be aware of your body language.** You want to stand up straight and smile.
- **Don't cross your arms in front of your chest** or put your hands on your hips. Use some hand and arm gestures to punctuate your presentation, but go easy on them. You don't want to look like you're drowning and waving for help.
- **Stand with one foot slightly forward.** This will help to keep your body steady as you speak.

Ask for Feedback

Have questions ready to ask your test audience when you finish.

What do you think the thesis of the presentation was?

Did I make a convincing argument?

Was there anything I discussed that you found confusing?

Did I vary my tone and facial expressions?

Ask them to tell you what they remembered from your presentation. This will give you clues as to what parts of your presentation are getting the audience's attention.

TIP FILE

If you have a time limit, look for ways to practice knowing what, say, fifteen minutes of public speaking feels like. Put a watch on the desk or podium while you practice, and glance at it. Or keep one eye on the clock at the back of the room.

Now, Revisit and Revise

Now that you have tried your hand at practicing presenting, it's time to figure out how to turn your first draft into a final draft. You want to add style and sparkle, and polish, polish, polish. Fortunately there are a number of ways to take your presentation up a notch.

The first place to start is with the opener. Take a look at how you started your first draft and think about how you can make it more engaging.

For example, look at how this opening was revised to capture the attention of the audience:

ORDINARY	EXTRAORDINARY
Today I am going to talk about teenage drinking and how advertising encourages it. According to Webster's Dictionary, Fifth College edition, alcohol is defined as . . .	Alcohol is killing the youth of America. That's what Gillian Kelcher writes in her Web summary Teenage Drinking in America.

Kick Off with a Quotation

You can quote one of your sources for use as your opener, an expert in the field, or a famous wit—

"A fool and his money are soon elected."
—Will Rogers (1879–1935)

If you quote someone who's not necessarily associated with your topic, make sure you connect the quotation back to your subject and your point of view. For the quotation to work effectively, it needs to be apparent to your audience why you're using it.

If you want to shake the audience up a bit, try quoting someone you think is all wrong. Then go on to show why this person is so off the mark. Keep in mind the effect you want to create on your audience and the quotation's relationship to your presentation as a whole.

Remember, the source of the quotation matters. Trying to explain why a new product was delayed, a speaker said, "Anything worth doing is worth doing slowly." His face turned red when someone pointed out the source of the quotation—the famous striptease artist Gypsy Rose Lee.

Nothing is more boring than hearing the same old quotations, so be creative in your search for quotable material. Song lyrics, advertising copy, and even comedians can provide good quotations. Proverbs can be useful, too, as can the tag lines, or catch phrases, from well-known advertising campaigns, if you can find a way to give them a proper twist—Homework: Just Do It. The French Revolution—I'm Lovin' It.

Try Some Humor

Many people think the only way to begin a presentation is with a joke. But jokes are hard to choose, hard to tell, and hard to move on from.

Gentle humor works as well as, if not better than, jokes with a punch line. One speaker began by quoting to his audience some translated signs he'd seen in hotel lobbies.

> "Please enter the lift backwards and only when lit up," said one.
>
> "Please leave your values at the desk," said another.

The audience laughed, and the speaker launched into his talk on preserving important company values, even in tough economic times.

Humor Without Hurt

You want to be funny, not cause pain (or not very much pain, anyway). Here's how to stay in the safe zone:

Joke about yourself. A short cabinet secretary used to say he did not represent big government.

Joke about things that don't matter. You can always make jokes about the weather or the climate. "How hot is it in Las Vegas, anyway?" But don't be insensitive. Tsunamis are not funny, as hosts of a morning radio show found out when they played a song making fun of the victims of the 2004 disaster.

Joke about what people make fun of themselves about. Everyone used to kid Ronald Reagan about his age—even Ronald Reagan. When Hillary Rodham Clinton ran for the Senate, she made jokes about how many black pantsuits she had—because that's what she always wore.

Ask a Question

Get your audience thinking from the get-go. Pose a question, such as the following:

- What drove the United States to enter World War II?
- Why are hunting licenses being issued for buffalo in Montana?
- Why is the wolf still on the endangered species list?
- Why aren't women allowed to play major-league baseball?

When you open with a question, you get your audience involved. But make sure the question is interesting and relevant. Test-drive it on some people you know. If it starts a lively conversation at the lunch table, you know you've got a good one. If your friends say, "Who cares?" you'd better keep looking—or find new friends.

Tell a Story

Everyone likes to hear a good story, and that's why anecdotes—short accounts of interesting or humorous incidents—make such effective openings. Keep your eyes and ears open for interesting stories as you prepare your presentation.

ORDINARY	EXTRAORDINARY
This guy once told me that it's not what the other guy does, but what you do that counts in a fight.	"I heard a prize fight manager say to his fellow who was losing badly, 'David, listen to me. It's not what he's doing to you. It's what you're not doing.'" *—Bill Cosby*

State the Facts

They say that knowledge is power, and sometimes factual information can make for a dynamic opening. For example, for your presentation on teen drinking, you might employ one of the following facts to help make your case:

- According to government statistics, at least eight million American teenagers use alcohol every week, and nearly half a million go on a weekly binge—that is, have five or more drinks in a row.
- Junior and senior high-school students drink more than one-third of all wine coolers sold in the United States—that's 31 million gallons—and more than 1 billion cans of beer each year.
- The U.S. Department of Justice reports that almost one-third of young people who commit serious crimes have consumed alcohol just before doing so.

A string of surprising facts can make your audience hungry to hear more.

Look for astounding statistics. While researching, did some piece of information make your jaw drop or seem impossible? What startles you is likely to grab your audience's attention, too. Remember to round off numbers.

INTERESTING FACTS FAST

Try ***Harper's Magazine***, which publishes Harper's Index each month. You can also find it at **http://www.harpers.org.** The index publishes a statistical snapshot of the world's economic, political, and cultural climate. You'll find things like the number of Avon ladies in China (more than 15,000) or the average amount that Americans spent on candy for Mother's Day in a year (nearly $5 per mom).

Timely Transitions

There are numerous ways to make transitions from one part of your presentation to another.

Use single words to move from one idea to another. These include "and," "but," "however," "although," "because," and "since." You can also create internal summaries to help listeners know where they are—"Now that you are aware of the dangers of drinking and driving, let's look at ways to avoid it." Occasionally, take a break and be quiet for three to five seconds. Use the time to look around the room or at your notes.

Use "first," "second," and "third," or "first," "next," and "last" as transitional phrases. Change your volume and tone of voice. Saying "right" or "okay" with emphasis signals listeners that you are moving to a new topic.

And finally, use body language. You can step forward, smile, pause, and begin anew. You can rearrange your note cards while you pause. Begin your next sentence loudly, emphasizing the first word. This will help to get your audience's attention. Use a quotation to segue from one topic to the next. Use an anecdote to move from one subject to the next.

TIP FILE

Here are a few things to keep in mind when creating a fact-based opening:

Round off numbers. The exact amount of money spent by Americans for Mother's Day candy was actually $4.70. "Nearly five dollars" is easier to say and to hear.

Make size easy to understand. If you're explaining how small something is, compare it to the width of a human hair. Explaining how large it is? Compare it to a two-story building or the Statue of Liberty.

Extraordinary Endings!

A good ending does a lot of work in an oral presentation. It reviews the information you've presented, as well as its importance. It can suggest ways to get more information on the subject. It lets the audience know the presentation is complete.

Think of your presentation as a circle—the closing should come around to connect again with the opening. This will make the presentation feel whole and well constructed, and it will leave a good impression in your listeners' minds.

Here are some ways to close:

- If you began with a question, restate it and provide the answer.

Does a good president have to have military experience? Judging from the examples of Lincoln, Wilson, and Franklin Roosevelt, the answer is clearly no.

- If you opened with an anecdote, refer to it once again. Tell how things turned out, or how they might have turned out differently if your plan had been adopted.

Without mandatory drug testing, innocent students like Melissa would not have to suffer needlessly.

- If you began with shocking facts, tell how the action you propose could alter those statistics.

If alcohol companies could be compelled to change their tactics and stop appealing to young people in their advertisements, teenagers would drink less, their overall health would improve, and the incidence of violent crimes would decrease.

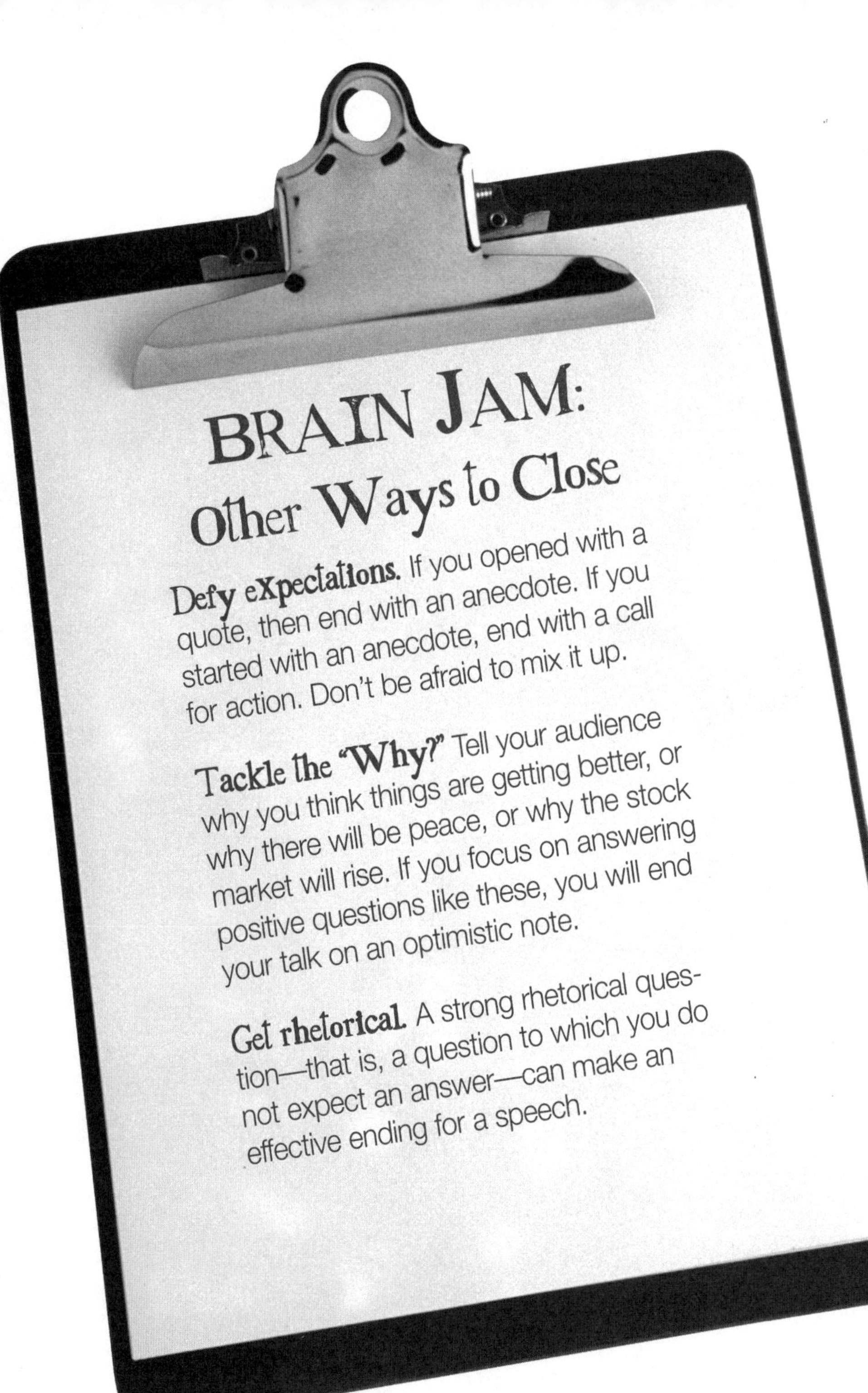
BRAIN JAM:
Other Ways to Close
Defy eXpectations. If you opened with a quote, then end with an anecdote. If you started with an anecdote, end with a call for action. Don't be afraid to mix it up.
Tackle the "Why?" Tell your audience why you think things are getting better, or why there will be peace, or why the stock market will rise. If you focus on answering positive questions like these, you will end your talk on an optimistic note.
Get rhetorical. A strong rhetorical question—that is, a question to which you do not expect an answer—can make an effective ending for a speech.

Models

The local

Maps and char

Conversations

albums

DVD

Albums on

PowerPoint slides

multimed

THE SPIN ROOM

Using Multimedia!

Using Multimedia!

If you want to do an average presentation, simply standing up in front of the class reading from note cards might be okay. But to give an extraordinary presentation, you'll need to be more creative to drive your point home and capture your audience's attention.

Music and Other Audio Elements

You can use music to set the mood or to make a point if the lyrics to a song relate to your topic. You can open and close your presentation with a brief piece of music, such as the theme song from *Star Wars* for a report on high-tech weaponry.

PowerPoint Presentations

More and more teachers are asking for students to create presentations using presentation software programs, such as PowerPoint. That way, you work on your computer skills while developing your presentation talents.

Using software programs like PowerPoint allows you to add color, graphics, art, photographs, and other visual elements to your presentation. These programs generally offer a selection of background colors and designs, choices of fonts, and excellent tools that enable you to create effective outlines.

TIP FILE

If you tend to get nervous, using video clips, PowerPoint slides, and other visual materials is a great way to get everyone focused on something other than watching you giving your presentation.

So Here's the Scoop

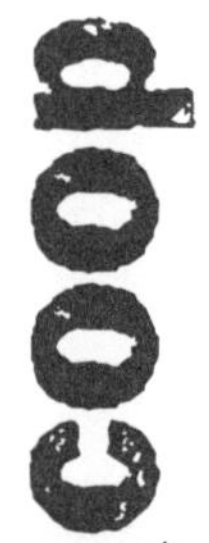

Here are some suggestions for tackling PowerPoint and slide presentations:

Limit the number of points per page as well as the amount of information each page contains. Three or four points is about the limit. Less really is more.

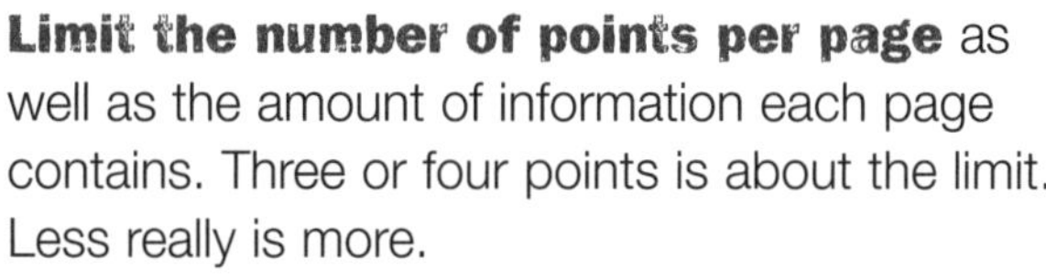

Use bullet points to prompt your memory, illustrate with an example, and summarize.

Don't put your whole text on a slide. If you want the audience to have your text, print it and hand it out after you're finished.

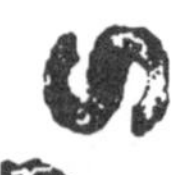

Avoid flashiness. You want the focus to be on your presentation, not how cool your slides are.

Use a single font throughout, and use large type. Don't use all capital letters. They're harder to read.

Background patterns and graphics make slides harder to read. If you use a background, make sure it is subtle.

Complex graphics are distracting, so keep them as simple as you can.

Use no more than one graphic or visual element per slide.

Video Clips

A great, short video clip can inject more life into your presentation. The audience can see firsthand the issue you are trying to persuade them to accept, believe, or support. If your presentation is about the importance of recycling, show your audience a video of a rain forest being destroyed.

The Internet is a great source for video clips. Type "video clips," rain forest into **http://www.google.com,** for example, and you'll get literally thousands of hits, from kissing toucans to tapirs. Make sure the video actually adds to your presentation. If it's a diversion or a time filler, leave it out.

Posters, Handouts, and Other Visuals

Even if you don't have the latest in technology, there are still ways to jazz up your presentation.

Posters. If you are doing a presentation on an author, you might create a poster or enlarge a cover from one of his or her famous works to display while you talk. You can use word-processing programs to print out the type for your poster and graphics programs to create images. Color copies and scanned photos can be included, too.

To start putting together a poster, decide on your main message. Craft a headline that tells your story. Next, figure out how much space you have, and roughly lay out your words and pictures. Put the most important message in the center top position—that's where your headline goes. The information should then go from most to least important.

Classroom props. Even props that are already in the classroom can be used. You've looked at that map on the wall a million times. It would be a great tool to show your audience where the Battle of Normandy took place or where the last remaining Siberian tigers live. Use the board to write out your main points, to write out equations, or to draw diagrams.

Handouts. Want to give your audience a take-away? You can print up the outline of your presentation or your speaker notes and give each person a copy. Or consider handing out a list of suggested reading for those who want more information. Hand these out at the end of your presentation. You don't want the audience shuffling through papers when they should be listening to you.

Troubleshooting: Common Problems

Unfortunately, even the best-prepared presenters can run into trouble. One of the most common challenges is the battle of the clock.

What If It's Too Long?

Respect the time limit. It's a part of your assignment, and how well you manage it may be a factor in your grade. Never exceed your time limit by more than a few minutes.

Find ways to trim down your presentation. Cut extra words, clauses, and phrases. Get rid of loose adjectives— "pretty," "nice," and "very" are among the most common and the most easily cut. Adverbs, too, can often go— "beautifully," "strongly," and the like.

Review the number of points you're trying to cover. Go back over your outline and see what you can afford to cut. Dispense with some minor points. It will make your main points clearer. If you've quoted four facts, maybe the strongest two will do.

What If It's Too Short?

Again, respect the time limit. Yes, Lincoln's Gettysburg Address is a model of brevity, but he wasn't getting a grade. So get ready to add more meat. Think in terms of ideas, not extra words. You don't want to put lots of verbal filler in your presentation or become repetitive. You want to add new ideas or content, not fluff.

You can accomplish this in several ways. One way is to elaborate on what you've got. Look for facts you can explain in detail. Add more than just words. Add detail that's interesting.

You can also add a quotation or anecdote. If it's a book report, add a quotation from the book. If it is a science report, add the story of how the invention was made, or quote from a scientist's laboratory journal.

A sign of an extraordinary presentation is its ability to answer any questions that the listener may have on the subject. This can also be a great way to make your presentation longer. Write a list of possible objections that someone might have to your take on the subject and incorporate answers to those objections into your talk.

What If It's Dull?

Examine the language in your presentation.
It might be helpful to record your presentation and listen to your words.

Play with the rhythm of your words and sentence structure. Inject life into your talk by using active verbs and strong nouns. You want the language itself to be dynamic and engaging.

You also want to make sure you're being as specific as possible. General statements are never as powerful as detailed ones, especially those anchored in fact.

Punch Up Your Language

To counteract boredom in your listeners, use fresh language and lively examples.

ORDINARY	EXTRAORDINARY
My friend Steve has three tattoos.	A green snake wraps itself around my friend Steve's left arm. On his shoulder, there's the flag in living color—red, white, and blue. And on his left wrist, Steve's got a heart that reads "Mother."

The extraordinary example creates vivid images in the listener's mind instead of the flat, informative ordinary example. Look for ways to invoke the listener's five senses during your presentation.

GET WORD SMART

With the help of a few reference books, you can improve your writing and up your word IQ. There are a number of books dedicated to helping you wipe out clichés:

The Penguin Dictionary of Clichés by Julia Cresswell

The Facts on File Dictionary of Clichés by Christine Ammer

Not sure whether you should use "affect" or "effect"? There are several books aimed at helping you sort out confusing words:

The Dictionary of Confusable Words by Adrian Room

A Concise Dictionary of Confusables: All Those Impossible Words You Never Get Right by B. A. Phythian

What If It's Too Complicated?

You've practiced for friends, and they are scratching their heads. You've lost your audience with complex concepts, too much information, or a confusing structure. Remember that people are listening to—not reading—what you've got to say. Make it easier on their ears.

You can sometimes make things complicated when you're not sure what you're talking about. Make sure you know your subject cold. If not, go back and clear up any misunderstandings you might have.

Look to simplify your language. Use simple sentences and change words to make them simpler. For example, substitute "start" or "begin" for "initiate." Don't utilize when you can use.

To the Podium!

Okay, the big day is here. Your presentation is on schedule, you've done all your preparation and practice, and you're ready to go.

Here are a few extra hints and tips:

- Use an outline or note cards or use your PowerPoint presentation as a kind of guide.
- Clip your outline pages or note cards together so that when you go up to speak, you won't drop them.
- Number cards or pages boldly at the top center so you'll know you're on the right card right away.
- If you're using a computer, a slide projector, or overheads, plan to arrive early to make sure your equipment works.

HELP WITH VISUALS

Looking for help with a computer program that creates visuals? Want to learn how to scan images into your computer or create a poster for a science fair presentation? Check out the University of Alabama's great Web site, **http://bama.ua.edu/~hsmithso/class/bsc_695/links/index.shtml**.

You'll find links to sites that will help you with digital images and editing, making graphs, drawing and animation programs, and making slides, overheads, and posters. While the site is geared toward scientific presentations, the advice and information is useful for presentations of all kinds.

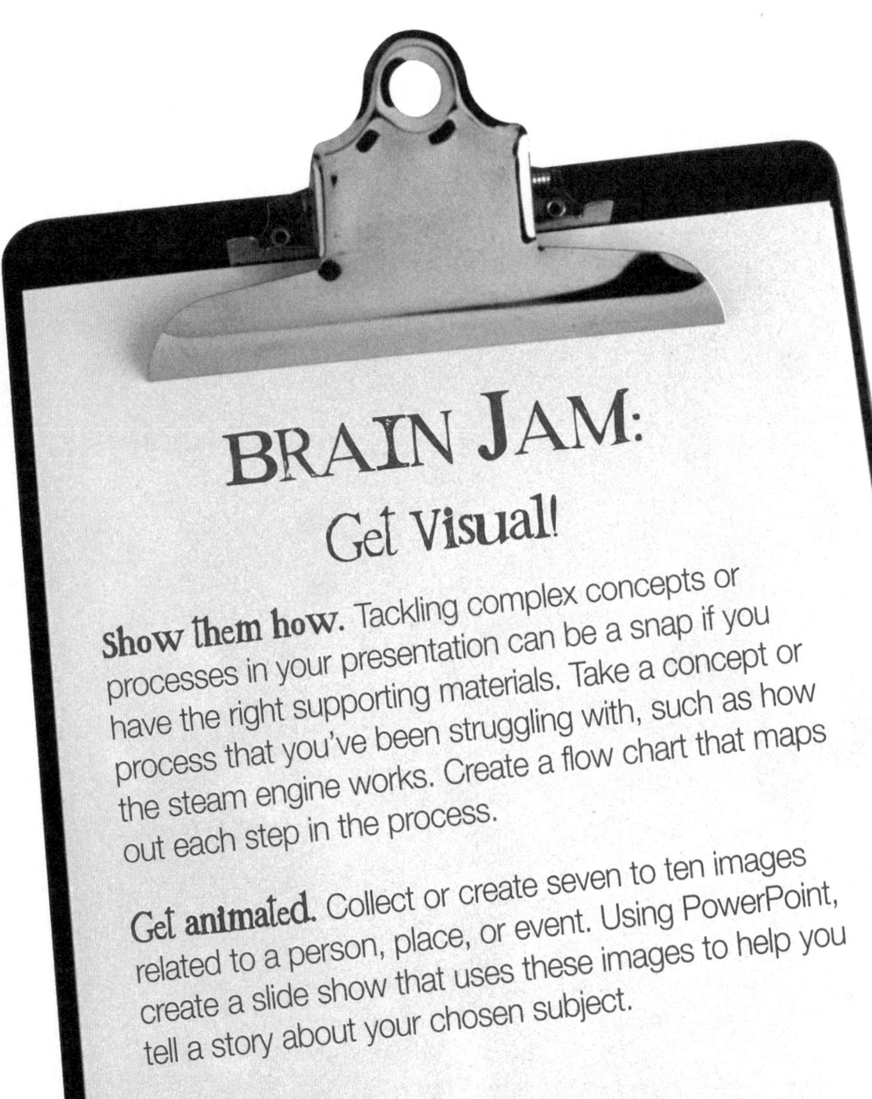

BRAIN JAM:

Get Visual!

Show them how. Tackling complex concepts or processes in your presentation can be a snap if you have the right supporting materials. Take a concept or process that you've been struggling with, such as how the steam engine works. Create a flow chart that maps out each step in the process.

Get animated. Collect or create seven to ten images related to a person, place, or event. Using PowerPoint, create a slide show that uses these images to help you tell a story about your chosen subject.

Find an angle, o

pick a topic you

anguage that

e, or a PO

ell a story.

Introdu

A GUIDE TO PRESENTING PERSONAL EXPERIENCES

Not Your Average Summer Vacation

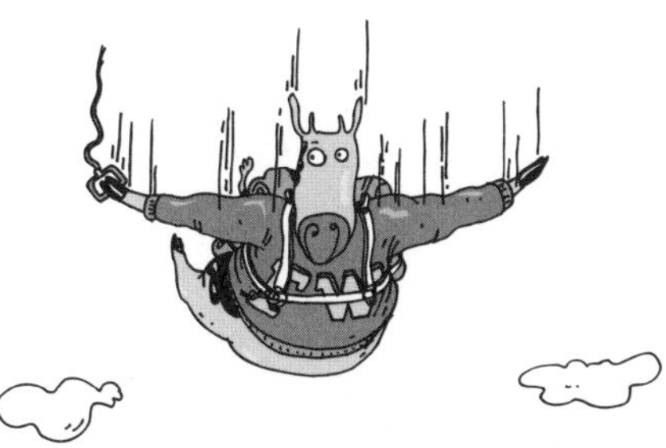

point of view.

interesting char

A Guide to Presenting Personal Experiences

If you're asked to give an oral presentation on a personal experience, **your main purpose is to inform, and possibly to entertain.** You'll be telling a story about something that happened to you. But your teacher will be looking for more than a list of sights you've seen. You'll be expected to be able to talk about what your experience meant to you. What did you learn about life from your trip to Europe? How did that week in the car with your little sister change the way you feel about her or about yourself?

To begin, pick a topic, narrow it down, and find an angle. Of course, it helps to pick a topic you like. Your family's trip to Walt Disney World last summer will make a good subject, but only if you had a good time or a terrible time. If it was dull, can you really turn it into a good talk?

What if you've never gone anywhere? You can tell exciting personal experience stories anyway. Think about something that touched or troubled you. Peer pressure situations make good stories, because everyone's exposed to peer pressure, and everyone's interested in how to handle it. Think about any activities you do in the community. Have you done any volunteer work? Maybe you helped out on a coat drive for the homeless or worked in a soup kitchen, and it gave you fresh appreciation for all that you have. Can you talk about how helping others showed you something about your own life?

Keep in mind that experiences like these make great college application essays. Come up with a good story for this assignment, and you're sure to be able to use it again.

Pick an Angle

You need to determine your focus. Maybe your visit with Mickey Mouse made you realize you're not a kid anymore. Maybe you met a family from another country and realized that, in spite of obvious differences, you shared many of the same traits.

Even a personal experience presentation needs a strong thesis statement.

ORDINARY	EXTRAORDINARY
My Trip to Disney World	*It's a Small World After All*
A Trip to France	*French Breakfasts— What's Not to Like?*
I Quit the Debate Team	*No More Arguments for Me*

Make Connections, Give Details

Talking about yourself is tricky. **Your challenge will be making your story come alive for the audience.** You were there, so you already know the details and, if you're not careful, you're liable to skip over some important ones.

You won't need to do much research, but you will need to do some. How deep is the Grand Canyon, anyway? And how do geologists think it formed? These would be interesting facts to use in your talk about your summer visit there.

Introduce an interesting character or several. Make sure we meet the individuals who made the experience memorable. If these include members of your immediate family, be sure you tell the audience something about them. Don't assume we know them as well as you do. For example: "Emily, who is eight, can't stand hamburgers, while Jesse, who's eleven, never met a slab of beef he didn't like. You can imagine what a stop at McDonald's turned into. . . ."

TIP FILE

Look for ways to share your experience with your audience. If your presentation is about a trip, show a map highlighting your route or video clips of the people you encountered. Type up a recipe that's central to your talk and share copies of it with your class. You can even take a page from late-night television and create your own top-ten list of things you learned from your experience.

What's Your Point?

Be sure to go beyond the specific incident being covered in your talk. Maybe you learned something about life from the way your aunt taught you to bake baklava. Maybe you learned some important lesson when you got lost but then managed to find your way home. Be sure to point out the broader lesson to your audience.

Strike a balance between telling what happened and relating the story to more abstract ideas. If, for example, you're telling about the Japanese family you met in Florida, you'll want to introduce us to the family members and describe them, but you'll also want to tell how they were different from you, how they were like you, and what you learned about life from your time together.

Extraordinary personal experience presentations clue the audience in to the larger importance of the event as well as paint a vivid portrait of what occurred.

READ ABOUT IT

One way to get a better feel for speaking about personal experiences is to read how others have tackled telling their own stories. There are several nonfiction collections available that include teens talking about their experiences. Here are two examples:

The Courage to Be Yourself: True Stories by Teens About Cliques, Conflicts, and Overcoming Peer Pressure, edited by Al Desetta

The Struggle to Be Strong: True Stories by Teens About Overcoming Tough Times, edited by Al Desetta and Wolin Sybil, Ph.D.

PROJECT JUMPSTART

Think about a family activity. Do you cook with your father? Go surfing with your grandmother? Pick one and examine what you've learned from your family members through this shared activity.

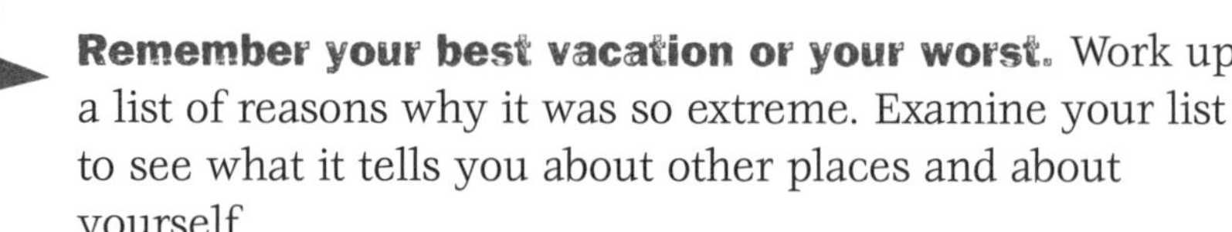

Remember your best vacation or your worst. Work up a list of reasons why it was so extreme. Examine your list to see what it tells you about other places and about yourself.

Get physical. Relate an experience you had with sports. This could be what it felt like to be picked last for basketball or how playing football made you better at math.

BRAIN JAM:
Appeal to the Five Senses

Create a verbal snapshot. Write a paragraph describing what one scene in your presentation looked like. You want your listeners to be able to see the French café at dawn, the sun rising over the sea in Key West, the darkness inside Space Mountain.

Provide sound cues. Go through your subject and find five sounds that might be overheard if the listeners had been with you. Mention a few sounds your listeners might hear, such as waves crashing on rocks or cheers from the crowd, to help them get a better feel for the setting of your presentation.

Lead them by the nose. Pick three pleasant scents (a freshly washed T-shirt, for example) and three unpleasant scents (fumes from a nearby sewage treatment plant) and describe what memories and/or associations you make with each smell.

Provide some flavor. What is the most unusual food you've ever eaten? Chocolate-covered grasshoppers or sugar-coated chili peppers? Pick two or three odd eats you've had and write a short description to describe what the food tasted like.

Add texture to your talk. While it's great to tell your audience what things might look like, it's also important to let them know what things might feel like. Look around you and pick three items. Describe how each of these items would feel, too.

Communicate the
issue and why it

State yo

ls of

ell why you chose

problems and of

Discu

A GUIDE TO PRESENTING HISTORY

Who, What, Where, When, So What?

A Guide to Presenting History

Making an interesting history presentation often means taking a fresh look at the old stories. In the recent past, many historians have begun to look for fresh angles—telling the history of the Civil War from the point of view of the women who stayed home or became camp followers, or from the perspective of the men who fought and died.

Finding an interesting angle can be as simple as choosing a fresh perspective on an old story and seeing how the facts look through someone else's eyes.

When choosing your topic, look for this fresh point of view. If you're assigned to talk about the Battle of Trenton, for example, could you tell the story of that battle from the point of view of the Hessian soldiers who were surprised at the Old Barracks? If you're asked to give a presentation on the Crusades, could you explore the subject from the Arabs' point of view?

Support Your Thesis

Whatever topic you choose, be sure to state your thesis clearly. In most cases, your thesis will often be the conclusion you reached at the end of your research:

> *Joan of Arc may have dressed in men's clothing, but she was no feminist.*
>
> *George Washington won the Battle of Trenton through a combination of skill and dumb luck.*
>
> *For the Europeans, the Crusades were fights to win back the Holy Land. For the Arabs living in the Holy Land, the Crusades were a barbaric invasion.*

Once you have your thesis, use all your tools to tell your story effectively. Describe people and places, quote directly from primary sources, and recount anecdotes you encountered in your research. And be sure to begin with a dramatic moment. Maybe you've read an account of a drunken soldier waking up to the sound of gunshots on Christmas morning, or you've come across an account of the Crusaders entering the Holy Land from an Arab boy's point of view. Keep digging until you come up with a beginning that will grab your audience and make them want to hear more.

Don't Forget the "Why"

Extraordinary history presentations tackle the "why" as well as the "who," "what," "where," and "when." You want to let your audience know why you chose your topic.

> *"I've heard about the Hessians, but I wanted to know more—who were they, why were they fighting, what did the battle feel like to them, and what happened to them afterwards?"*

Perhaps you've read two contradictory reports of the Battle of Trenton and wanted to learn the truth. Or maybe you weren't satisfied with the most popular explanation of a historic event. Sometimes, current events, such as U.S. involvement in Iraq and the rest of the Middle East, can make a topic like the Crusades exciting again.

Research Is Key

Research is especially important in a history presentation, so make sure you discuss the sources that you consulted. Where did you find your evidence? Did you interview survivors of the hurricane or read newspaper reports from the time? Did you come across the diary of a Civil War soldier in a used bookstore? Primary sources are usually required for historical oral presentations. If you are allowed to use secondary sources, do so sparingly.

You will often need to interpret the sources you discover, which can be fun.

One student, writing about the Middle Ages, examined a copy of a warehouse inventory. From the materials that were listed—including flax, cotton, wool, and many different kinds of dyeing herbs—she was able to conclude that the town had been an important textile center during the Middle Ages. Her own interest in weaving and her familiarity with dye plants and fibers made the research fun for her and the presentation fascinating for the audience.

To make her presentation even more extraordinary, she could have shown some bills of sale showing the movement of goods into and out of the warehouse. For your presentation, try to find and analyze several accounts of a historical event.

Differing Points of View

Your research may indicate that different people saw the event or activity in different ways. A study of the slave trade in the Americas during the 1700s, for example, should include the economic viewpoint of the slave traders, the human misery of the slaves, and the moral indignation of religious sects such as the Quakers.

If accounts of an event differ, discuss why. This is where secondary sources can be useful. You can turn to experts to see if one source is deemed more reliable than others, for instance.

TIP FILE

Draw in your audience by incorporating visuals into your presentation. Show a video clip of a battle reenactment or scan in photographs of key figures mentioned in your presentation and add them to your PowerPoint slides. Make these events and people real to your audience.

Outlining History

As you prepare your outline, here are some additional points to consider:

- What is the central issue at the heart of the project, and why is it important?
- How did the scope of your project change over time? Did you begin with one set of assumptions, only to discover new evidence that sent you off on a different tack?
- Did you come up against any problems as you did your research? Were sources missing, or were parts of pages torn? Did people die before they could be interviewed?
- How did you overcome any problems you encountered in your research?
- Are there questions that remain to be answered or problems still to be solved?

Be prepared to answer questions about your investigation. It helps to repeat the questions before answering them. This gives you time to think about the answer and lets everyone in the audience know where you are going.

PRIMARY SOURCES

Many primary sources have been made widely available through the Internet. For instance, if you're looking for information on the Battle of Trenton, try the Web site **http://www.theamerican-revolution.org**. Here you will find not only the date of the battle (December 26, 1776) but also the weather (about 20 degrees Fahrenheit, winds calm), the number of casualties on each side (5 for the Americans, 107 for the British), and the battle commanders on both sides. You will find a synopsis of the battle, suggestions for further reading, and even an eyewitness account of the battle—a primary source!

Another Web site, **http://www.americanrevolution.org**, includes valuable material about the Hessians based on original material destroyed during the Allied bombings of World War II. The book was published in 1884, but it's a great source for anyone wanting to know more about the mercenaries who fought and died in America for Great Britain, not for principles but for their prince's paycheck.

PROJECT JUMP START

Explore a historical period through the experiences of lesser-known figures. For example, what was it like for a child laborer working during the Industrial Revolution?

Find a pioneer. The life of one groundbreaking figure can provide an interesting angle on an entire historic period or event. The work of Martin Luther King, Jr., can shed light on the nonviolent civil-rights protests of the 1960s.

Play with time. Look at a particular day in an important battle instead of an entire war.

"History does not repeat itself.
The historians repeat one another."
—Max Beerbohm (1872–1956)

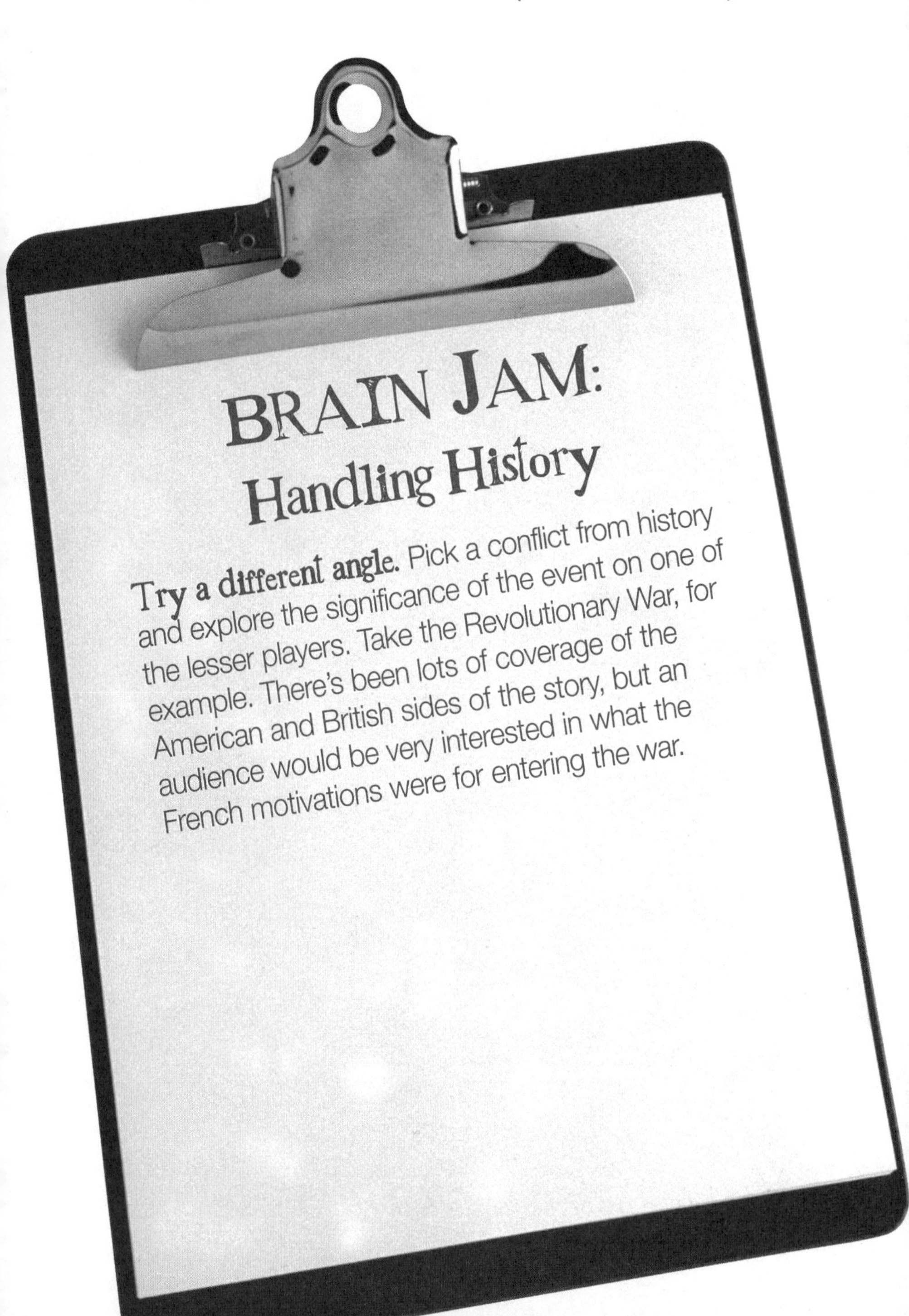

hink about the p

Consider t

Choose your boo

Talk abo

Make notes.

the theme

Ask yourself,

A GUIDE TO PRESENTING LITERATURE AND POETRY

I Read It, Really I Did

A Guide to Presenting Literature and Poetry

Talking about books, stories, and poems can be fun. That must be the case, because millions of Americans belong to book clubs, where they get together and make presentations on what they've read. Of course, no one's making them read ***Moby Dick***. But even your assignment can be pleasant if you know how to go about it.

Assess Your Assignment

Before you begin an oral report on literature, make sure you know how long it should be, when you're presenting, and what points you are expected to cover. If you're assigned a book, story, or poem, look it over to see how long it is and what the general topic might be.

If you get to choose, pick something you like. Make sure you have time to read the whole thing and still prepare your oral presentation by the due date. Don't try to read something really long if you're a slow reader and you have lots of other assignments.

"What is written without effort is in general read without pleasure."
—Samuel Johnson (1709–1784)

Read It!

Now it's time to read the book, play, poem, or story. **Really read it.** Sit down in a quiet place where you won't be interrupted, and let the book work its magic on you. If you've read it before, reread it to get familiar with it again.

Don't rely on plot summaries, Cliff Notes, your mom's memory, or a Classics Comics version. You may get the plot, but you'll miss the nuance. The use of language is important in literature; you've got to read the original if you want to get a good grade.

Don't think that seeing the movie is the same as reading the book, either, although you might liven up your report by comparing a movie and a book of the same title. How does the movie version of ***Jane Eyre*** differ from the novel? For a really classic take on the kinds of changes books undergo to make their way onto the silver screen, try reading one of the books in the ***Lord of the Rings*** trilogy and comparing it with the film version.

TIP FILE

Avoid reading a written report out loud. This is an effective way to put your audience to sleep. You want to sound natural, not overly formal or stuffy. If you've already written the report and have to present it orally, make sure you convert the text to an outline that you can speak from easily.

Note-taking

Make notes while you read the literary work or when you reread it. Here are some things you'll want to include in your presentation:

- Title of the book, short story, essay, or poem
- Name of the author
- The year the book was written. It helps your audience to know when ***Catcher in the Rye*** was written, or when Jane Austen lived.
- What kind of writing is it? Fiction or nonfiction? If it's fiction, is it a thriller, science fiction, or a historical romance? If it's nonfiction, is it history, biography, science, memoir, or an essay? If it's a poem, is it an epic, a lyric, or a dramatic monologue?

"What we want is a story that starts with an earthquake and builds to a climax."
—Samuel Goldwyn (1892–197

TIP FILE

Once your report is ready to deliver, take a copy of the book with you when you go up to speak. If you want to quote passages from the book, have the pages marked. You can use sticky notes to mark the page and the approximate point in the text.

Get Creative with Literary Themes

One essential piece of your literary presentation is theme. In other words, what's the piece of writing about? You may wish to begin by stating the theme of the piece in the beginning.

Here are some examples:

ORDINARY	EXTRAORDINARY
Pride and Prejudice is about getting married.	*Pride and Prejudice* is a book about marriage and family, but it's mostly about the ways in which we form snap judgments about other people that are frequently wrong.
The story of *Moby Dick* focuses on Captain Ahab's search for a whale.	*Moby Dick* is a book about whaling, but it's also about obsession.
The poem "My Last Duchess" describes a woman featured in a painting.	Robert Browning's poem, "My Last Duchess," is about a woman, but it's also a psychological portrait of a cruel and murderous man.

Give Important Details, Set the Scene

Next, you might talk about the book's setting and the main characters.

Setting. For instance, if you were reporting on ***Moby Dick,*** you could say that the book begins in Nantucket, but most of the action takes place aboard a whaling ship at sea. The action takes place in the early to mid-1800s. You can use drawings, maps, and background information to help your audience understand the importance of Nantucket to the whaling trade, for instance, or what a moor is.

Main Characters. To understand the action of a novel or short story, we need to know who the actors are. The main characters of the novel include the narrator, Ishmael; Queequeg, the Indian; Captain Ahab; and the whale, Moby Dick. Ahab and Ishmael are almost opposites—a fact that might give you an idea for your report. Comparing and contrasting main characters is a good topic for an oral report on a novel or story.

Managing the Plot. You should briefly summarize the plot of the book, but don't give it all away. Don't retell the story in detail. It might help to remember that most novels and short stories are written in five basic parts:

1. **The exposition lays out the basics of the tale**—who's involved, what it's about, where it's happening. In ***Moby Dick***, the exposition lays out for the reader who Ishmael is and why he is going to sea. This section sets the stage for the action.
2. **The second section—the rising action—can be a large part of the story.** In ***Moby Dick,*** there are many adventures, including the meeting of Ishmael and Ahab, the dread that overcomes Ishmael when Ahab describes the aim of the voyage, meetings with various ships, and a typhoon. These events and others constitute the rising action and help to get the reader involved.

3. **The climax, the third section, is usually the most intense part of any book or story.** In ***Moby Dick***, the climax includes the main chase and the battle with ***Moby Dick***. It lasts for three chapters and covers three days.

4. **The falling action is usually relatively brief within a novel or story.** In this part, the author is beginning to wrap things up. In ***Moby Dick***, the description of Ahab's death and the sinking of the ship go pretty quickly, but this section explains a lot about the meaning of the story.

5. **The final section of a novel or story, the resolution, really does wrap things up**. In ***Moby Dick,*** for example, Ishmael tells us in the resolution that Ahab's madness means little in the grand scheme of things. Another ship, the *Rachel*, rescues the remaining surviving sailors, and the tale is over. When talking about the resolution, make sure to provide an accurate description of important outcomes.

If you use these five parts of the novel to discuss the plot, you will cover the most important material. You may not want to give away the ending of the story if others in your audience have not read the book. Instead, you could hint at what happens. For example:

> *Although the* Pequod *doesn't return to shore, Ishmael and others survive to tell the story.*

You Read It, So What Did You Think?

Along with your analysis of the text, you'll probably need to say what you thought of the book and why. Here are some suggestions to keep in mind.

Give your overall impression of the piece of writing.

> *Although* Moby Dick *was funny and interesting at some points, overall I felt it was boring and way too long.*

As in any oral presentation, give specific examples of what was boring, and which sections were too long.

How did it make you feel?

> *I felt like I learned a lot about whaling by reading* Moby Dick.

What was the best part?

> *I especially like the description of Queequeg's tattoos, because it showed me that tattoos were an important means of self-expression hundreds of years ago.*

Would you recommend it to others? If you liked it, be specific. Did you like the plot? The main character? The setting? The kinds of language the author used?

If you read a poem, did you like that a poem rhymed or that it didn't? Did you like the sounds of the words or the rhythm? Either way, be specific. Sum up how you felt about the work.

PROJECT JUMP START

Make connections. Study the life of the author as well as his or her other works. Can you find links between life events and his or her writings? You may even want to create a time line showing the relationship between the two.

Examine facts in fiction. Find a fictional work about a famous event and look at its portrayal of history. Is it accurate? How does the author incorporate historical information? What kinds of details does he or she use to establish the setting and the time period?

BRAIN JAM:

Get Literary!

Sum it up. Take a look at a popular novel and check out the back cover. Most times you will find a short summary that indicates what the story is about without giving away all of the plot twists and turns. Write your own version based on a literary classic you once read for class.

Be a poetic listener. So much of the power of poetry has to do with how it sounds. Take one of your favorite poems and see if you can find some of the following poetic devices:

Alliteration: This refers to the repetition of same consonant sounds. For example, the phrase "safe and sound" repeats the "s" sound.

Onomatopoeia: This refers to a word that imitates the sound of the item it refers to—for example, "sizzle" or "boom."

Rhyme: This refers to words that have similar sounds. Sometimes in poetry, you will find that similar sounds are repeated at the ends of lines.

Use logic and e

both pros and

Decide how you'll orga

Answer objectio

close forceful

Read around.

A GUIDE TO PRESENTING HOT TOPICS AND CURRENT EVENTS

Pro Versus Con

A Guide to Presenting Hot Topics and Current Events

Read any newspaper or watch the news on any two television stations, and you'll be aware that there are at least two points of view on any subject. Hot topics are those that arouse strong feelings or are the subject of much debate. In current events, issues such as war, taxes, assisted suicide, and the privatization of almost anything from toll roads to social security can set off furious debate. Every subject area has its own hot topics, too. Law enforcement, ecology, sociology—in every discipline there's a point to be made, either pro or con, on almost any issue.

Suppose you're called on to give an oral presentation on a current event or on a hot topic in a particular field. All the suggestions on giving an extraordinary oral presentation apply, of course, but there are some special hints that might help you get through to your audience.

Here are some hints on choosing your topic and doing research:

- **Try to pick your own topic.** It's easier to argue for something you feel strongly about. If you're presenting on a current event, you'll probably have to present both sides of the issue. The pros and cons, say, of building a new stadium for your town's football team will be easy to talk about if you actually give a darn.
- **Read widely about your topic.** Articles in magazines and newspapers usually turn out to be the best sources for information about current events and hot topics. Look for data, charts and graphs, and quotes you can use.
- **Make a list of pros and cons as you read.** If you're making note cards, prepare a stack of pros and a stack of cons.
- **Go through your notes and answer any objections.** Let's say your subject is animal testing. One side says it hurts and kills hundreds of animals each year. How do you answer that? Maybe you say that this type of testing is necessary to advance medical research and mention some key discoveries found through animal testing.
- **Write answers to all the pros and all the cons,** making up new cards for the opposite pile.
- **Rhetorical questions, facts, and challenging assumptions work** well for openings when talking about hot topics and current events.
- **Don't forget about using quotations and humor.** Check humor Web sites (or go to **http://www.about.com** and look at its political humor section) to get an idea of what others are saying about your subject. Humor works especially well in presentations like these. Hot topics are things that make people angry, and humor can go a long way toward diffusing the heat.

Organize Your Thoughts

The main objective of this type of assignment is to see how persuasive you can be. You want to win listeners to your side.

Try stating the topic, then go through all the reasons for supporting one side, then all the reasons to support the other. That will work if you are being asked to report on both sides of an issue. However, if you are required to take a stand for one side or the other, make it clear which side you're on in your thesis statement. Then state each objection and your rebuttal to it.

Use logic and emotion when making your arguments for or against an issue.

> *"Yes, putting up more traffic lights will cost money. But how can you put a dollar value on the lives it will save?"*
>
> *"Of course no one wants to torture animals, but testing pharmaceuticals on animals is an important safeguard and aids in saving human lives."*

Close forcefully. You might end by summing up all the reasons you've chosen one side or the other.

If you're required to summarize the pros and cons of a situation, you might point to ways in which the disagreement could be resolved, or point to a proposed plan that seems like it would solve the problem—for example peace talks, a new contract that gives workers more rights and more responsibilities, or the implementation of a new policy.

Again, Research Is Key

It takes a lot of research to make this type of presentation extraordinary. You want to research your topic thoroughly to avoid encountering any surprises during or after your presentation. Make sure you collect evidence for and against your position.

Along with facts, look for quotations to help sway your audience. For example, for a presentation on electronic voting, this quotation attributed to Joseph Stalin could deliver quite a punch: "Those who cast the vote decide nothing; those who count the vote decide everything."

Even if a quotation isn't specifically on the subject, it still can be helpful. Mark Twain once said, "The difference between fact and fiction is that fiction must be believable." This quotation was used by former Texas congressman Jim Hightower in talking about the issue of electronic voting. His essay on the subject (available in a slightly condensed form at **http://voteamericavote.com**) is a model of how to make a good argument. His conclusion on how to make electronic voting machines a viable option is to require a voter-verifiable paper trail to be kept of every vote in every election.

TIP FILE

If your position changes based on your research, you might include that information in your talk:

"I was all for computerized voting machines until I read about what happened in Ohio in 2004 . . ."

What changed your mind might change those of others.

Build Your Case

What if you were having an argument with a friend on the electronic voting topic? Write down all the things you'd say, such as the following:

- Where computerized electronic voting machines have been used, a number of incidents have made the election outcome questionable.
- Computerized voting can't be checked, so it's possible for software to get the totals wrong (possible flaws in the system).
- It's been shown that some voting machines—especially the Diebold system—can be hacked from outside (fraud is possible).

Organize your statements in a logical order, building your case as you go.

The beginning of your outline may look like this:

I. Possible flaws
II. Possible fraud
III. Historic problems
IV. Possible solutions

Once your outline's in order, use the facts you uncovered in your research to support each argument you put forward.

Write a Powerful Opening

Sometimes the most powerful type of opening is a story. Cesar Chavez, a well-known leader of the farm workers' labor movement, sometimes started his speeches with an anecdote to illustrate the issue at hand. When talking about the hazards of pesticides, he told a crowd:

How do you measure the value of a life? Ask the parents of Johnnie Rodriguez. . . . Johnnie was a five-year-old boy when he died after a painful two-year battle against cancer.

His parents, Juan and Elia, are farm workers. Like all grape workers, they are exposed to pesticides and other agricultural chemicals.

Chavez is able to employ this example as a springboard to talk about the health problems associated with pesticides and to make a case for farmers to stop using them. Along with anecdotes, unusual facts and engaging quotes are ways to make your presentation extraordinary.

End on a Strong Note

Remember: it is often the last thing you say that stays with your audience. One of the most memorable closers came from a presidential inaugural address. President John F. Kennedy ended his speech with a call to action: "My fellow citizens of the world, ask not what America will do for you, but what together we can do for the freedom of man." Review your notes for powerful facts or quotes or try your hand at crafting a dramatic closing of your own.

PROJECT JUMP START

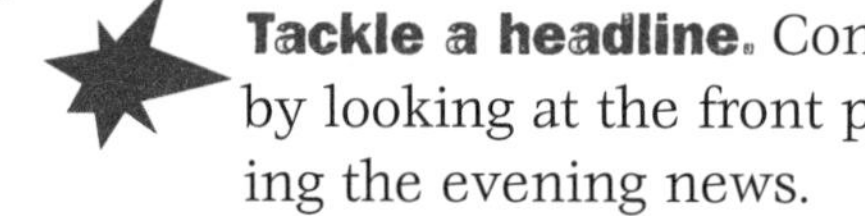

Tackle a headline. Controversial topics can be found by looking at the front page of a newspaper or watching the evening news.

Explore a social issue you've encountered personally. Whether it happened to you, a friend, a family member, or someone you know, having a direct connection to a social issue, such as eating disorders, genetic testing, or job cutbacks, will lead you to create a more substantial presentation.

Explore a global problem and look at its effect on your community. Sometimes it helps your audience to understand a problem, such as global warming or air pollution, when they can see its impact on their own lives.

BE A CRITICAL THINKER

Creating an extraordinary presentation on hot topics and current events requires strong analytical and critical-thinking skills. Here are a few books to give your brain a workout:

The Newspaper Reader: Reading, Writing, and Thinking About Today's Events by Seth Frechie, Harold William Halbert, and Charlie McCormick

Asking the Right Questions: A Guide to Critical Thinking, Seventh Edition by M. Neil Browne and Stuart M. Keeley

Good Reasoning Matters! A Constructive Approach to Critical Thinking by Leo A. Groarke and Christopher W. Tindale

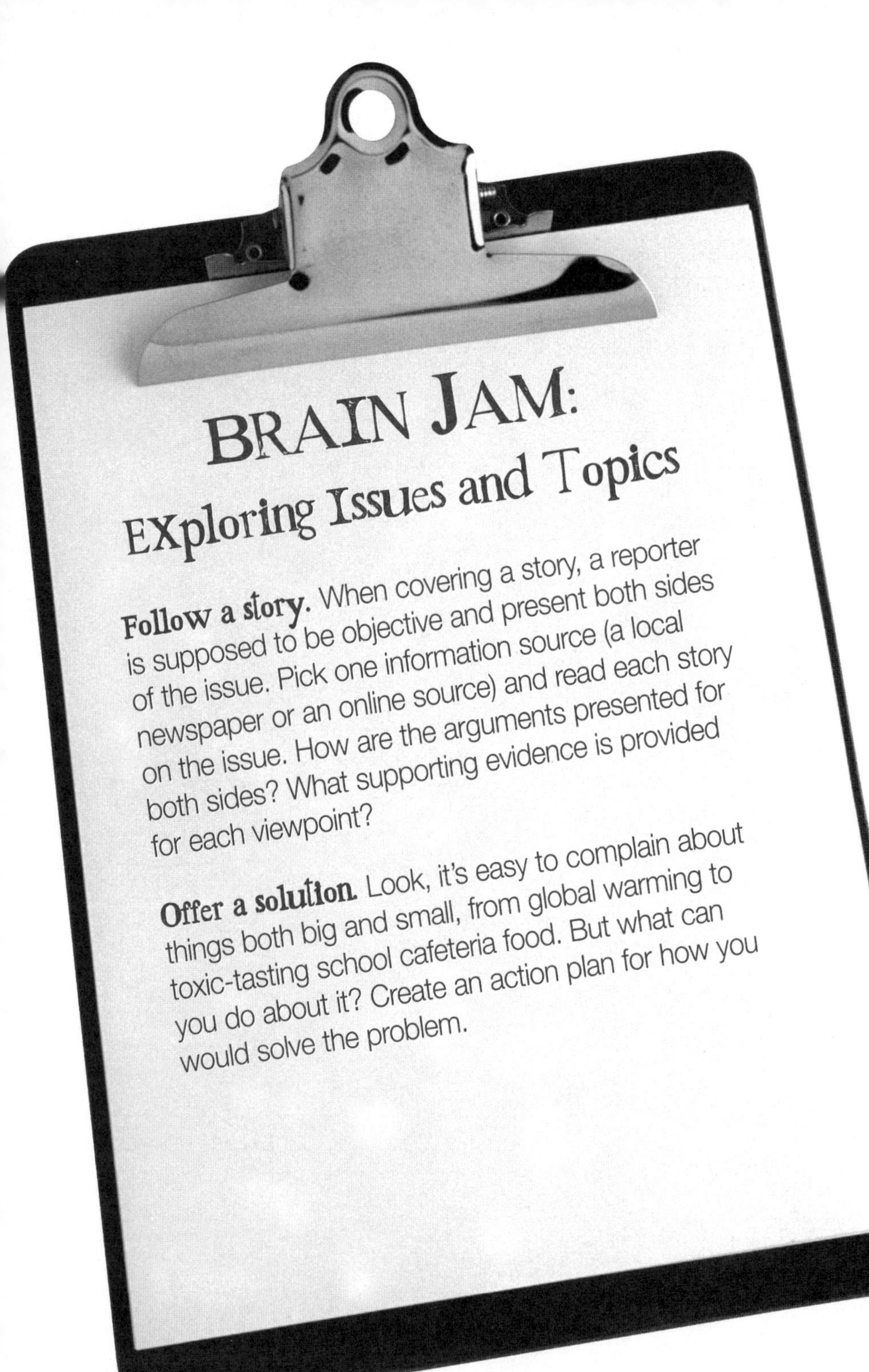

BRAIN JAM:

EXploring Issues and Topics

Follow a story. When covering a story, a reporter is supposed to be objective and present both sides of the issue. Pick one information source (a local newspaper or an online source) and read each story on the issue. How are the arguments presented for both sides? What supporting evidence is provided for each viewpoint?

Offer a solution. Look, it's easy to complain about things both big and small, from global warming to toxic-tasting school cafeteria food. But what can you do about it? Create an action plan for how you would solve the problem.

set the agen

Ask your

n a description and a p

State th

Use graphics and charts to make your data clear

Describe your met

Share your conclu

Go for a strong finish

A GUIDE TO PRESENTING SCIENCE TOPICS

The World Isn't Flat

A Guide to Presenting Science Topics

Even scientists have trouble making oral presentations about science. Many are very involved in their research but lack the skills they need to communicate their findings to a wider audience. Yet making presentations is a crucial part of the scientific life. Many Ph.D. programs in science require students to take a course in oral presentation, because students will find themselves speaking to their peers, to general audiences, and to financial backers more often than they know.

While the same rules that apply for oral presentations in other disciplines hold true for scientific presentations, you might have more difficult concepts and terminology to wrangle with during your talk.

Outlining a Scientific Presentation

The path to an extraordinary science presentation is a straight line. Scientific presentations seem to go best when they follow a straightforward outline. Tell the audience what you are going to talk about, giving them a peek at what's to come. Then present detailed findings and come up with a strong close.

To begin, tell your audience briefly what you will talk about, and give them an outline of your talk. You might want to use visuals and show bullet points listing your main ideas.

"Today I want to explore the topic of starfish. Last summer I saw quite a few in tide pools formed near a jetty at Barnegat Light."

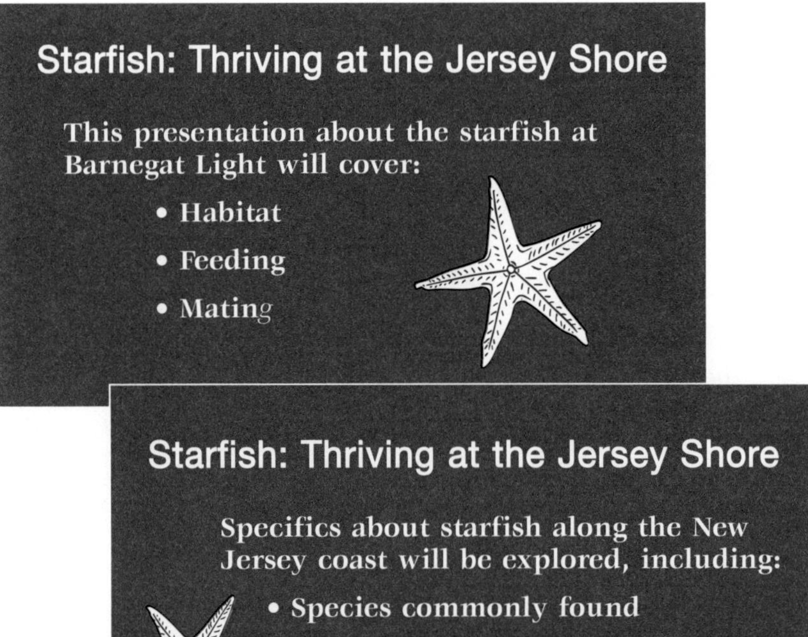

Once you have given a brief summary, ask your key question or state your hypothesis. Questions can help focus your talk. For example, you might ask how large the starfish population is or whether there have always been starfish along the New Jersey coast.

While you talk, you will want to let the audience know about your discovery process. Describe your methods very briefly. How did you set out to answer your question? Did you talk to marine biologists, read articles in science magazines, or spend your summer days counting a particular population of starfish? Whatever methods you used, tell your audience about them, but don't go on for too long. It can be boring to listen to sixty days of meticulous notes taken on the beach.

Tell the audience about the results of your experiment or research.

"Although the gulls seemed to find starfish delicious, over the course of the summer, I actually saw an increase in the number of starfish at Barnegat Light."

"Marine biologist Sherman Stringer told me that the starfish population in New Jersey is declining rapidly from year to year."

Significance of Findings

Extraordinary scientific presentations do more than just reveal results; they let the audience know the significance of the findings. Make sure to share your conclusions about what your findings mean. This is really the heart of your talk, so be a little more expansive here. If you've found, for example, that the population is increasing, explain why. Is it because global warming is creating a more hospitable climate for the starfish, or because their predators are dying out? If you've found that the population is under attack, explain what's wrong and how it might be corrected.

In your closing, be sure to acknowledge anyone who helped you in your research. If your mom drove you to the beach every day or a marine biologist spent an afternoon speaking with you, acknowledge them. If you cited published works, be sure to acknowledge their authors.

Using Analogies

Because not everyone is familiar with scientific terms and concepts, you may find yourself telling your audience things they've never heard before. How do you make it easy for the audience to understand?

When Neil Armstrong stepped onto the moon, he said the surface was covered with fine dust. Trying to describe it, he said, "When you put your scoop in, it smoothes it out, just like plaster." Armstrong was using an analogy—telling about something unknown (moon dust) by comparing it to something known (plaster). Try using analogies to explain concepts that are foreign to your audience. Use similes and metaphors to make material clear. Tell your listeners what something is like.

Special Challenges

Writing or talking about science poses some special challenges. Many times, you'll be introducing new concepts, information, and ideas to the people in your audience. You'll have to make sure you're communicating clearly by presenting the information in a way that's easy to understand. Remember, your listeners won't have your text in front of them. While visual aids can help you make some points simpler, here are other hints for getting your points across:

- **Define terms.** Don't assume your audience is familiar with the concepts that form the basis of your talk. Outline these concepts briefly, but clearly, early in your presentation.
- **Summarize your hypothesis in two or three sentences.** That way, you'll be able to restate it for your audience.

- **Tell a story.** Think of your investigation as a mystery, and get your listeners involved early. Your presentation will be more fun to give and to hear. For instance, if you're talking about those starfish, begin with your discovery of the mysterious creatures and your wonder at their appearance, and move on from there. You should have the audience interested in your investigation.
- **Stay focused on the important facts,** and avoid irrelevant details.
- **Avoid using jargon whenever possible.**

The conclusion of a scientific presentation is very important. It's your take-away message to the audience. It's what they will remember of your talk.

Try to end your talk with a strong, clear statement. For example, *"Scientists expect that as more reefs are built along the coast, the starfish population will continue to increase. So at least for now, the starfish of New Jersey seem safe."*

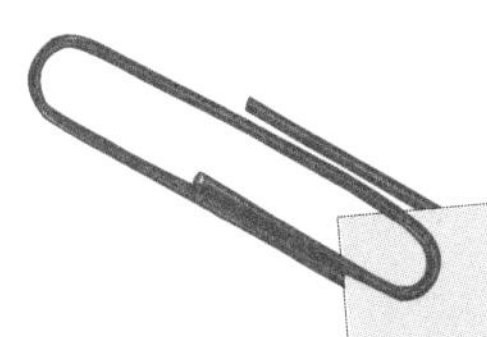

TIP FILE

One of the best ways to take your presentation to the next level is to provide lots of supporting materials. In the case of scientific presentations, charts, diagrams, and other illustrations can make tough concepts easier to understand.

PROJECT JUMP START

Unravel a natural phenomenon. Your audience most likely has seen news reports about the effects of hurricanes and tornadoes, but they may have very little understanding of how and why they happen.

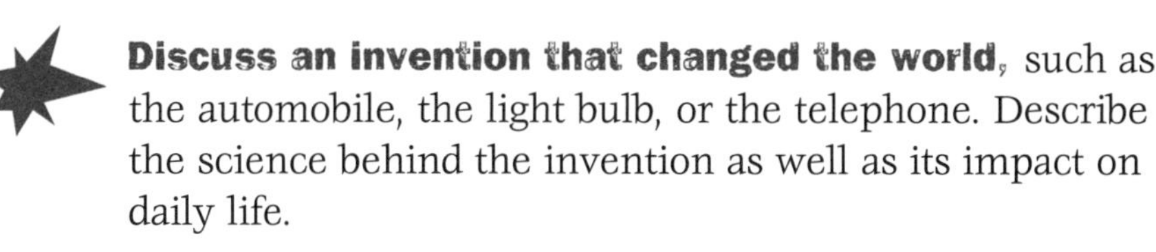

Discuss an invention that changed the world, such as the automobile, the light bulb, or the telephone. Describe the science behind the invention as well as its impact on daily life.

Tackle a scientific process that people encounter almost every day. How do they get the bubbles into soda?

BRAIN JAM: Picture This!

Hang it up. Pick a key concept in your presentation and make a poster to show how it works. Remember to think about the students in the last row as you design your poster. They should be able to see what's going on. Any writing should be large and clear. Use numbers and arrows to label the steps and show the flow.

TO FIND OUT MORE

Books

Bartlett, John and Justin Kaplan. *Bartlett's Familiar Quotations: A Collection of Passages, Phrases, and Proverbs Traced to Their Sources in Ancient and Modern Literature, 17th Edition.* Boston: Little, Brown, 2002.

Bernard, André and Clifton Fadiman. *Bartlett's Book of Anecdotes, Revised Edition.* Boston: Little, Brown, 2000.

Boller, Jr., Paul F. *Presidential Anecdotes*. New York: Oxford University Press, 1996.

Caroselli, Marlene. *Great Session Openers, Closers, and Energizers: Quick Activities for Warming up Your Audience and Ending on a High Note.* New York: McGraw-Hill, 1998.

Newstrom, John W. and Edward E. Scannell. *The Big Book of Presentation Games: Wake-Em-Up Tricks, Icebeakers, and Other Fun Stuff.* New York: McGraw-Hill, 1998.

Vilord, Thomas J. *1001 Motivational Quotes for Success: Great Quotes from Great Minds.* Cherry Hill, NJ: Garden State Publishing, 2002.

Organizations and Online Sites

A Bit Better: PowerPoint Tips
bitbetter.com/powertips.htm
This site has helpful hints on making PowerPoint presentations.

A1 Free Sound Effects
http://www.a1freesoundeffects.com
This site has a limited number of free sound effects from a variety of things.

American Rhetoric: Online Speech Bank
http://www.americanrhetoric.com/speechbank.htm
This site has an audio and video library of speeches from a variety of sources.

Bartleby.com
http://www.bartleby.com
This site is a fantastic one for finding quotations and reference materials. It has online encyclopedias and other reference texts to fulfill basic research needs.

BrainyQuote
http://www.brainyquote.com
This site has quotations on a variety of topics and subjects.

Clipart Connection
http://www.clipartconnection.com
This site has a wide variety of clip art that can be downloaded for free. There are photos, clip art, animations, and more for use in your presentation.

Clip-art.com
http://www.clip-art.com
This site offers free clip art.

ESpeeches.com
http://www.espeeches.com
This site is a resource for tips on giving speeches. It also has an audio library of speeches for students to listen to.

GoodQuotes.com
http://www.goodquotes.com
This site has a variety of quotations.

History Channel
http://www.historychannel.com
This site has audio and video clips of important people and historical events.

Library of Congress
http://www.loc.gov
This is the Library of Congress's official site. There is a lot of reference material available on this site, including audio, photographs, and more.

Quotations page
http://www.quotationspage.com
This site has a database of quotations by and articles about writers and other topics.

Quoteland.com
http://www.quoteland.com
This site has quotations on a wide variety of topics. It is an excellent source for finding quotations and doing research. There is also a reference library on this site.

Index

ABOUT THE AUTHOR

MARGARET RYAN

Margaret Ryan has written speeches for executives in the businesses of fashion, finance, travel, and technology. When she's stuck for an idea, she usually cruises the Internet looking for quotations or tries to come up with a great story to begin the speech. Her favorite part of speechwriting is helping bland bureaucrats develop sparkling speaking personalities.